Further Praise for Lisa Marie Nelson's ...g There!

"*Since I consider parenting to be the most important profession in the world, and family the foundation for the future, I strongly recommend that all parents and all those who expect to be parents read and re-read Lisa Marie Nelson's* Getting There!"

—John Wooden, author of *They Call Me Coach*

"*Lisa Marie has written a wonderful book that will enrich the lives of individuals and their families. She skillfully blends her own thoughts and feelings about ways to find fulfillment in life with the inspirational words of many renowned people. Lisa Marie's ideas are so simple, yet so powerful. Her suggestions are realistic and achievable. This book is a gem and I am certain that it will be read and re-read on numerous occasions. Each reading will provide new insights to help us lead a life characterized by spiritual nurturance and love.*"

—Dr. Robert Brooks is a clinical psychologist on the faculty of Harvard Medical School and the author of *The Self-Esteem Teacher*

"*What a wonderful handbook for parents to combine practical day-to-day life with rich, spiritual values. This book is a treasure!* Getting There! *offers parents bite-sized nuggets of practical spiritual wisdom to feed a child's spirit, nourish a child's mind, and inspire a child's positive future.*"

—Diane Loomans, author of *Full Esteem Ahead* and *The Lovables*

"*This is an important book that speaks to the reader. It may change your life. This book has enriched my soul, fed my spirit, and opened my heart. Lisa Marie Nelson has the biggest heart of anyone. And it's written all over these pages. This book will make you feel more lighthearted. This is a lighthearted good read that will nourish your spirit.*"

—Cheryl Sindell, author of *Cooking Without Recipes*

"*Lisa Marie has written* the book *for the new millennium. A society is only as good as its families and, right now, ours are in pretty ragged shape. In a world full of neighborhoods without sidewalks and Columbines splashing across our television screens at an ever-increasing rate, we search for answers. They can be found in our very homes. Reconnecting with the holy in our lives is the surest way to rebuild the foundation of our society. Lisa Marie's book* Getting There! 9 Ways to Help Your Kids Learn What Matters Most in Life *is a wonderful instructional book on how to rebuild our lost structure.*"

—Scott Stantis, creator of *The Buckets* comic strip and syndicated
award winning cartoonist for *The Birmingham News*

"*At a time of increasing spiritual malnutrition,* Getting There! *is a family feast. Sit down with those you love and partake. Your heart will thank you for it.*"

—Paul Pearsall, Ph. D., author of *Wishing Well:*
Making Your Every Wish Come True

Getting There!

9 Ways to Help Your Kids
Learn What Matters Most in Life

Lisa Marie Nelson

JOURNEY
EDITIONS

An imprint of Tuttle Publishing
Boston • Tokyo • Singapore

First published in 2000 by Journey Editions, an imprint of Periplus Editions (HK) Ltd, with editorial offices at 153 Milk Street, Boston, Massachusetts 02109.

Copyright © 2000 Lisa Marie Nelson

Library of Congress Cataloging-in-Publication Data

Nelson, Lisa Marie.
    Getting there! : 9 ways to help your kids learn what matters most in life / Lisa Marie Nelson. −1st ed.
        p. cm.
    ISBN 1-885203-82-9 (wire-over)
    1. Family − Religious life. I.Title

BL625.6 .N45 2000
291.4'41−dc21

99-048865

Distributed by

USA
Tuttle Publishing
Distribution Center
Airport Industrial Park
364 Innovation Drive
North Clarendon, VT 05759-9436
Tel: (802) 773-8930
Tel: (800) 526-2778

Canada
Raincoast Books
8680 Cambie Street
Vancouver, British Columbia
V6P 6M9
Tel: (604) 323-7100
Fax: (604) 323-2600

Japan
Tuttle Shuppan
RK Building, 2nd Floor
2-13-10 Shimo-Meguro, Meguro-Ku
Tokyo 153 0064
Tel: (03) 5437-0171
Fax: (03) 5437-0755

Southeast Asia
Berkeley Books Pte Ltd
5 Little Road #08-01
Singapore 536983
Tel: (65) 280-1330
Fax: (65) 280-6290

First edition
06 05 04 03 02 01 00   10 9 8 7 6 5 4 3 2 1

Design by HERMANI & SORRENTINO DESIGN

Printed in Hong Kong

Table of Contents

Acknowledgments

Thank you to my wonderful family for providing daily support and inspiration. John, Freddy, and Brian are all so loving, and so loved.

Thank you to my teachers, Louise Taylor, Sue Rubin, and Deepak Chopra for helping me gain insight into all matters spiritual. A big thank you to Thom Hartmann, a shining example to all of us and a dear friend whom I respect and admire so much.

Bouquets of gratitude to Michael Kerber and Jan Johnson at Tuttle and to "midwife" Caroline Pincus for bringing this book to life. Thank you also to the rest of the family at Tuttle who helped to take care of this baby! I feel so fortunate to work with such terrific people.

I especially thank God for this opportunity and experience. Thank You. Thank You. Thank You!

Foreword

by Thom Hartmann
Author of *The Prophet's Way* and *The Last Hours of Ancient Sunlight.*

For some reason, most books about spirituality and self-improvement are convoluted, thick, confusing, and often downright impossible (for the normal person) to follow or live out.

I've never been able to figure out why this is.

The Sermon on the Mount couldn't have run more than about fifteen minutes, judging from how long it takes to read. The Ten Commandments are only ten: while Moses had a tendency to get long-winded, apparently God does not. Even John said, "God is love," and that was pretty much that from his point of view.

The most important elements of spirituality, of living life, of being a good and decent human being are simple. Love others as you'd love yourself. Forgive others . . . and yourself. Don't kick strange dogs.

So here's this book that one of the most wonderfully straightforward, honest, and enthusiastic people I've ever known wrote: *Getting There.* And it's straightforward, honest, and enthusiastic!

You're going to love this book. You'll find yourself copying pages to stick on the refrigerator, or on the bathroom mirror. You'll hear yourself saying, "Yeah! I know that, but didn't realize I knew it!" over and over again. You'll feel that you can get There, too.

Because, of course, you can.

Introduction

Getting There!

Consciousness = energy = love = awareness = light = wisdom = beauty = truth = purity. It's all the SAME. Any trip you want to take leads to the SAME place.

– Ram Dass

"Are we there yet?" is the familiar cry when the family is out on a road trip. When we've packed up the car, or the minivan, as the case may be, we have a destination in mind. We know how to get where we're going because we can follow a map and road signs.

We're on a journey of another kind, daily, as we find our way along the spiritual path. We know where we want to go, individually and as a family, but do we know how to get There? We want our children to grow spiritually with a deep sense of connection to the family and to the Divine. And we want them to continue with clear direction on their spiritual path as they become self-sufficient.

It is a spiral path within the pilgrim's soul.

– Henry David Thoreau

So, here we are, pilgrims in this new millennium. We yearn for peace, for answers, for direction. Our spiral path leads us to look within, to a Higher Consciousness.

This book is divided into nine chapters. Throughout the book are quotes from various people from various times, all of whom have gained insight that they can pass on to us. There are also "Directions,"—ways to go, things to do—that we can take to help clarify their ideas and bring them to a deeper level of understanding. Choose the activities that fit your family best.

Every road trip has its attractions—places we want to stop and linger, notice and explore. In the back of the book, you'll find 165 word magnets. Throughout the book you'll find "Magnetic Attractions." Use the magnets to create phrases, messages, or little sayings that you and your family want to remember. They can relate to the section under the heading "Magnetic Attractions," or they can be about almost anything you want your family to think about. I give you suggestions for messages you might want to put up on your refrigerator. Or perhaps you'll want to purchase a small magnetic board for your breakfast table, or to place next to the telephone, or wherever else your family will come across the message often.

"The Heart is Home.
We're Together Forever
to Learn and Share
an Energetic Attitude of Gratitude."

I invite you to create your own attractions as well. There are quite a few words to work with, and some blanks on which you can write any other words you might want to use. Create a "slogan" for the day or week. Post a discussion topic before a family-night dinner. Create a family mantra to use before meals. Or a meditation topic to use when you tuck the kids in at night.

A brief apology: in order to make the most out of the magnet words, none of them have capital letters, so your messages might look a little odd.

Each of the nine chapters has a key word that represents a different step along our family spirituality journey. Put all of the key words together and remember this message…this is the way to go:

We can get There from here, and I'll show you how.

The heart in thee is the Heart of all.

– Ralph Waldo Emerson

1

Follow Your Heart

The tiny flame that lights up the human heart is like a blazing torch that comes down from heaven to light up the path of mankind. For in one soul are contained the hopes and feelings of all Mankind.

– Kahlil Gibran

The light in our hearts that shows us the way is love. Love is the basis for our families; it is the foundation of our spirituality. When you get down to it, love is all there is. When we live our lives in love, our hearts are open, free to give, receive, and express love.

Listen to your heart. It's your connection to God, to people, to the universe, and to yourself.

– Melody Beattie

Family is at the heart of the universe. This pulse keeps love flowing. We learn so much about love through the experiences of being in a family, and particularly, of being a parent. Even during pregnancy, and especially when that little baby is born, boy, do we learn about love. It's as if we feel things more deeply, our emotions are right on the surface. (I don't think I'm the only new mom who cried at long-distance phone commercials!) We are overwhelmed with this miracle that has touched our lives in such a personal way, and we are never the same again. There is even research that shows that the hearts of mothers and their infants tend to beat in unison. It's called "entraining." It's no wonder that so many mothers say that they have never felt closer to God than when they were giving birth.

As our children grow, and family life becomes more complex, it can seem like more of a challenge to feel this natural connection with each other. Our children become more and more distinct individuals who appear separate from us. We can remain close, because spiritually, we are all One. Age and distance are not factors when it comes to love. In this chapter we will explore some ideas for keeping the heart-to-heart connection alive within our families.

What is most needed is a loving heart.

– Buddha

Real love begins where nothing is expected in return.
— Antoine de Saint-Exupery, *The Little Prince*

Pure love is unconditional. That is, love for the sake of love with no expectations, no demands, no conditions. This is the way love should work in families; this is the way God loves us. The Bible tells the story of the prodigal son, who goes out in the world and basically comes home with nothing. His father greets him with love, and prepares a party in his honor. We are loved always, no matter what. We are loved just as we are. We don't have to earn God's love—we have it, completely.

Sometimes love is uncomfortable, so we don't readily identify it as love. It makes us think and feel and care when we might rather not be bothered. But it is all worth it. We have a choice: live in love or live in fear. Fear is the opposite of love.

Every situation we find ourselves in is an opportunity . . . to teach love instead of fear.
— Marianne Williamson

If we divide everything in the world into two piles, love and fear, and we know that all there really is, is love, then everything that is not love is a cry for love. What is anger? If it's not love, it's fear. Fear of what? Fear of lack of love. Anger is an outward demonstration of a call for help to fill that void that feels like a lack of love. It's the same for anything we would put in the "fear" pile.

As parents, it is our responsibility to respond with love. Lashing out in anger only creates more of the same. It's up to us to remain calm and centered and to demonstrate love. Love is the solution. Love is the answer. It's true in every case. Always.

I have a lot of things to prove to myself. One is that I can live my life fearlessly.

– Oprah Winfrey

When we live with and express love freely in the family, that love radiates out into the world. Love gives us confidence, so we can live our lives fearlessly. As parents, we strive to provide a love-filled home for our children. Love can get us through anything and everything! No matter how hard a day we've had at work or school, just knowing we will come home to a house filled with love makes it all better. This sounds simple, but love is powerful, love heals.

Directions: "Write your own love poems." Gather your family together after dinner (or anytime!) to write love poems. If you don't know where to start, use "Roses are red, Violets are blue . . ." and finish the rest. Remember that poems don't have to rhyme! Encourage your children to write about anyone they love – a grandparent, sibling, friend, parent, or even a family pet. Share your poems with one another. If you are musically inclined, put the poems to music and sing them. Encourage everyone in your family to write what's in their hearts.

Magnetic Attractions: "Love is the solution." Post a message on your refrigerator or magnetic board. "Love is the solution." Or, "Love is all there is." Remind your family that the message is there and meant for them.

Recognizing Emotions

*It is terribly amusing how many different climates of feeling
one can go through in one day.*

— Anne Morrow Lindbergh

Great is the man who has not lost his childlike heart.

— Mencius

We can all learn a thing or two from our children about expressing
our emotions. Children express feelings right when they feel them.
They cry when they're hurt and laugh when they're feeling good.
It's all right there at the surface, and it just comes naturally
bubbling out.

We adults don't have to be quite so demonstrative, but it is
important that we be in touch with our own emotions and
express them in some way rather than holding them back. We
all know what a price we pay for repressing our feelings —
physical aches and pains, depression, anxiety, anger, miscom-
munication, etc. Just being aware of how we feel will help us
to better deal with the situation and take care of ourselves.

As parents, we feel what our children go through. We can
literally feel their pain. When Freddy didn't get invited to a
friend's party, my heart was breaking for him. There was not
much that I could say to make him feel better, but just being
there for him and allowing him to be sad helped him get
through it.

It's okay to wear our heart on our sleeve. If we all did, wouldn't
the world just be a little bit sweeter?

The heart has its reasons which reason knows nothing of.
— Blaise Pascal

As great as children are at expressing themselves in the moment, they do need our help to recognize their emotions and put a name to them. We can model this kind of maturity by being clear about our own feelings. Think about the difference between saying "I am sad" and "I feel sad." "I am" statements should be reserved for our names and for words that describe who we are: responsible, reliable, joyful, peaceful, honest, loving, etc. When we're discussing emotions and remember to say "I feel . . ." rather than "I am . . ." we teach our children the difference between who we are and the ways we feel.

When we validate what our children are feeling, we also teach them to allow others to share their feelings. My boys, like all brothers, fight with each other. With boys, arguing and wrestling is a lot of times just recreation. When my children were younger and things would get out of hand, inevitably, one of them would start: "I hate you!" What do you say in such a situation? As parents, it's our job to help our children to clarify their feelings. Give them the words they need to express themselves. Rather than negate their feelings by saying: "No, you don't hate your brother," try saying: "It sounds like you feel angry at your brother. How can you let him know what he did that made you feel angry?" Sometimes we have to step in and play the negotiator until children are old enough to work out compromises on their own.

The human heart is vast enough to contain all the world.
— Joseph Conrad

Magnetic Attractions: "We are One family. " No one can be happy all the time. We need to teach our children and ourselves to be open to all our feelings. Magnetic messages might be, "Our hearts are open," or "We are One family," which can be comforting during times of family stress. Ask your children what feeling words they'd like to post.

We must also be there to help our children work through complicated feelings, fears, anxieties, and frustrations. In a family, we have the opportunity to give and receive comfort and empathy, and spiritually connect with each other when we really need to.

Directions: "Match expression and emotion." This exercise helps children to recognize and identify their feelings and emotions. It also helps with social skills by helping them to better understand when other people express emotions.

Get a stack of old magazines and cut out pictures of people's faces. Ask your children to see if they can find an emotion that matches the expression on each face. Glue the pictures to poster board and label them, or put each one on a 3x5 card with the emotion written on the flip side. Take turns guessing which emotion goes with which face. Make your own funny faces looking in a mirror and take turns guessing which emotion is being expressed.

Looking Within

All the wonders you seek are within yourself.

– Sir Thomas Brown

It is only with the heart that one can see rightly; what is essential is invisible to the eye.

– Antoine de Saint-Exupery, *The Little Prince*

When my children get the "gimmes," I have to help them put things in perspective. Yes, I have actually said, "You won't find inner peace for sale at Toys R Us ®. Think about it. What do you really want? And why do you really want it?" After some discussion, they usually figure out that they wanted this thing because it was the popular thing and their friends would give them attention. Attention pretty easily translates into love. So what they really wanted was love. And love is something they already have.

It's our job as parents to help our children understand that things don't bring the joy they seek. Things can bring them happiness, but only temporarily. And that's okay as long as they see it for what it is. The real joy, the lasting peace, comes from within.

 Directions: Write yourself a letter. Put the date on it, and include these questions with your answers: Who am I? Whom do I admire and why? What do I want? What do I want to have accomplished one year from now? Put the letter in an envelope and seal it. Put a date on the envelope one year from today and don't open the envelope until then. When you open it, see how much you've grown and changed in that time.

This is a good activity to do on your birthday or on New Year's Eve. For children, sometimes a year is too long to wait! You might want to do this with them on the first day of school and open the envelopes with them on the last day of school.

 Magnetic Attractions: "Express yourself." When anyone in your family is having a hard time making a decision (or any time at all) make a magnet message saying "Listen to your heart." And don't be afraid to "Express yourself."

Making Time to Just Be

You don't have to try. You just have to be.
— David Viscott, M.D.

God desires the heart.
— The Talmud

These days children are pulled in all directions the same way that we adults are. They've got school and homework and all kinds of after-school activities. The best thing that we can do to keep them from getting stressed-out is to build in time to just be.

Unstructured time when they can play or hang out, just be by themselves or be with each other will help to remind them to think of themselves and their spiritual natures.

Magnetic Attractions: "Just be." Put the message up and tell the children your favorite ways to "just be." Ask them theirs.

Directions: "Grow a Little Plant." On your next round of errands, buy a little flowerpot and some seeds. Then, get the children together for a planting. Have them fill the pot with fresh soil, then plant some seeds. Show them how to water correctly so that the seeds get a good drink without drowning. Place the pot in a sunny window. Have the children take turns caring for the seeds. Over the following weeks, gather them together often to watch as the seeds turn into sprouts and sprouts into plants. Get everyone involved in loving and tending these little growing things. It is such a joy to watch a little plant grow. Explain to them that plants need the same things to grow that we do: Love and attention.

Respect

So live that you wouldn't be ashamed to sell the family parrot to the town gossip.

– Will Rogers

In our home, family members must show respect for one another. With two boys who, like many boys their age, fight as sport, we have more than once had to explain exactly what this means. We make it clear that swearing is not a sign of respect, neither are name-calling or put-downs. Because we are clear, the boys know what kinds of behaviors are expected of them. They don't always behave the way they know they should, but they know that when they don't there are consequences, and they take the consequences.

Every family will have its own set of values to agree to and follow. Many of these will be unspoken, but others should be clarified so that everyone understands.

 Directions: "Take an Imaginary Walk." Close your eyes and take an imaginary walk with someone you trust. Have your friend lead you around and describe to you where you are. Listen to the sounds, feel the ground beneath your feet. You may hear the rustling of a tree, feel its trunk, smell its leaves. You can't see the tree, but your senses tell you it's there. What other senses can you use to appreciate the world around you?

Respect that this tree has a place in the world, and gifts to give. Everything and everyone is here for a purpose. Respect yourself and respect each other.

Intuition

Get the habit of hunching, then you will always be on the magic path.

— Florence Scovel Shinn

It is the heart always that sees, before the head can see.

— Thomas Carlyle

Families who are "in tune" with each other have a heightened sense of intuition. One person knows what another needs without being told. When we are in touch with our own feelings, it's easier to be sensitive to another's, and that's what intuition is: heightened sensitivity. It's not such a leap from sensitive to spiritual.

On those occasions when we pay attention to it, our intuition can be a great compass. If we feel out of sorts, like we're veering off the path, our intuition can give us some guidance. If we listen, our bodies actually give us a lot of information. Take some time every day to be quiet and listen to your heart.

. . . there is no prescribed route to follow to arrive at a new idea. You have to make the intuitive leap.

— Stephen W. Hawking

Each event in our lives has significance, everything has a purpose. There are no mistakes and no coincidences. Your intuition can take you to where you want to be by following certain events and "connecting the dots." Look at the "coincidences" in your life and see if you can find a pattern. Dates are easy ones to track. For example, in our family February 14 is a very special day. It's Valentine's Day, of course, the day of hearts and love, but it's also a day that holds significance for my family and for me, personally. On that day in 1979, I received a letter from UCLA saying that I had been accepted to the school. That brought me to Los Angeles. Two years later, on February 14, I met John, who is now my husband. On February 14, 1987, we moved into our home on Pathfinder Avenue, where we still live. I love this house, and I love that I found my way to "Pathfinder." We celebrate this day at our house and make a really big deal out of it. I love that February 14 is a holiday that celebrates love, and we use it as a day to celebrate all the love in our family. When something comes up, if there is a 14 attached, or a "214," I take it as a good sign. My intuition has not steered me wrong yet!

Magnetic Attractions: "Tune in." You can't practice intuition if you're not tuned in. Post the reminder: "Tune in."

You get your intuition back when you make space for it, when you stop the chattering of the rational mind.
    – Anne Lamott, *Bird by Bird*

Brian is the one in our family who seems to be the most naturally intuitive – he doesn't question his hunches. It's almost unfair to play some games with him because it's as if he can read our minds! One time, when we were playing Password, Freddy gave him the clue: "Fins." There are a lot of answers for that clue, most people would say, fish, feet, swimming, goggles, something to that effect. Brian said: "Catfish," and he was right! When we focus on spirit, we become more intuitive, and we can use our intuition to help us get There.

 Directions: Gather the family together after dinner. Find something from your room and put it in a box with a lid. Then get everyone to guess what is in the box, using only yes or no questions. Encourage everyone to take their time and listen to their hearts, their hunches. Count how many questions it takes before they get the right answer. Then switch off and have them put something in the box so you can guess. Count how many questions it takes you to guess what's in the box. You'll find that the more you play, the fewer the number of questions asked. The first "hunch" is usually right! Talk to your children about trusting their intuition.

Faith

Having a child is surely the most beautifully irrational act that two people in love can commit.

– Bill Cosby

Having a child is a tremendous leap of faith! We can't see into the future to know what the world will be like when our children, or our grandchildren are grown. We can only have faith that however things are, our children will handle it. We can help to strengthen their faith, as well, so that they value their spirituality. We can water their roots for them while they're young, and teach them to water their roots as they grow. It's an important part of teaching them how to take care of themselves, body, mind, and spirit.

Find the seed at the bottom of your heart and bring forth a
flower.

– Shigenori Kameoka

Magnetic Attractions: "Faith guides us." "Every day in every way." Having faith is trusting our intuition, it's listening to our hearts. It's understanding the difference between who we are and what we feel. Having faith is respecting our fellow travelers and respecting the place that each of us has in the universe. Having faith is knowing that we are loved, and that where we are, wherever we are, is home, because we belong.

2

It Leads You Home

Be it ever so beautiful. There is no place like home.
— Frank Baum, *The Wizard of Oz*

Our journey takes us to many places, with many experiences and many people. We are out in the world and are a part of the world at the same time. The farther we travel, the more we experience, the wiser we become . . . the more we find that our journey brings us home. Home to where our heart is, home where we belong. Our journey is a journey within.

The place we call home gives us a feeling of safety and comfort. Our home is our haven. It's a safe place where we can retreat. It's a place where we can just be and just be ourselves. Even the word "home" has a mystical, musical quality to it, very similar to the sanskrit word "om," meaning One and All. Home sweet home.

So how do we create homes that reflect our deepest values? We can make a home truly our own by adding personal touches throughout. Colors, decor, and collectibles in a home all say something about the people who live there. In our home, we like to display family photographs. We also hang up great homework papers and display the creations of the various artists in the house. This is one way to honor, respect, and encourage creativity!

> *The roots of a child's ability to cope and thrive, regardless of the circumstance, lie in that child's having had at least a small, safe place (an apartment? a room? a lap?) in which, in the companionship of a loving person, that child could discover that he or she was lovable and capable of loving in return.*
>
> – Fred Rogers (Mister Rogers)

Ideally a home should have at least one room where everyone can congregate. Our family room is the most well-used room in our house! If you don't have a family room, a den or living room, or even the kitchen can be a place for the family to gather and be together.

If at all possible, make sure that there's some private space for everyone, so that everyone can be alone when they need to be.

Magnetic Attractions: "Home is _____." Give everyone in the family a chance to fill in the blank and have their message posted for the day.

Directions: Keep a family photo album. When you get duplicate photos (lots of labs offer "twin pix") sort them out into photo albums for each of your children. Include notes and dates, funny things that happened. It's great for children to have their own photo albums that they can look at and remember fun times and happy memories. When they go off to college or move into their own apartment, they can take the albums with them and feel like they're taking a little piece of home.

You can also create mini-albums from family vacations or big events like a first communion or Bar Mitzvah. Craft stores now have all kinds of memory book accessories to help preserve photographs and make terrific presentations. Go with the children and let them pick out stickers and things to help personalize your albums. These make great gifts for grandparents who may live far away.

> Your children
> are not your children.
> They are the sons and daughters
> of Life's longing for itself.
> They come through you
> but not from you,
> And though they are with you,
> yet they belong not to you.
> You may give them your love
> but not your thoughts.
> For they have their own thought.
>
> —*Kahlil Gibran*, The Prophet

Expression

Live so that when your children think of fairness, caring, and integrity, they think of you.

— H. Jackson Browne, Jr.

Honesty's the best policy.

— Cervantes

How do we express ourselves? Do we come from a place of spirituality? Do we make our families the priority? Do we look for love in any given situation? Do we act differently at home than we do in public? These are important things to think about.

As parents we need to live the kind of life we want our children to lead. Children learn from our example. They're watching us all the time! They hear what we say, even when we're not talking to them.

Our children may not have the same interests that we do. They most likely will not have the same taste in music, clothes, or reading material. That's okay. Somehow, that's how the system works, as it has for generations. We are allowed to disagree with one another. We are allowed to go through this process as a part of our growth. We all eventually grow up and find our own way. It's inevitable.

Directions: Designate certain days on your calendar as "Family Days." I know families who manage to do this once a week! But even if you can work it in only once a month, do it. On the "Designated Family Day," everyone spends the whole day together. It doesn't matter what you do, but you have to do it together, as a family. Find new ways to express love for your family. Make a cake, even when it's not someone's birthday. Take a family vacation. Go to a sports event and root for the same team. Go for a walk together, or ride bikes. Have a picnic. Rent videos and send out for pizza.

There are three things we can give our children to let them feel loved and at home. We can give them these things anytime, anywhere, and best of all, they cost no money. These three magic things are: Attention, Affection, and Time.

Attention

If I ordered a general to fly from one flower to another like a butterfly, or to write a tragic drama, or to change himself into a sea bird, and if the general did not carry out the order that he had received, which one of us would be in the wrong?' the king demanded. 'The general or myself?' 'You,' said the little prince firmly. 'Exactly. One must require from each one the duty which each one can perform,' the king went on. 'Accepted authority rests first of all on reason.'

— Antoine de Saint-Exupery, *The Little Prince*

Parents are the accepted authority figures in the family. We must do our jobs well if we are to maintain that position of authority. If we start being unreasonable, then our children aren't going to listen to us or take us seriously. We need to pay attention to the needs of everyone in the family and not make unrealistic demands.

Paying attention can be a real challenge with so many distractions all around us every day. But it is so important that we know what is going on in our children's lives. Who are their friends? What are their interests? What is their schedule like? What foods do they like? What music do they listen to?

On a recent "Candid Camera" show there was a segment where parents who went in for a parent–teacher conference were greeted by a substitute teacher. The teacher would introduce herself and explain that she didn't really know the child, but would like to, and would ask the parents how the child was doing in school. This was actually a very interesting turning of the tables. Some parents had no idea what their child was learning in school or how they were doing. Other parents knew a lot about what was going on at school and how well their child was keeping up. They knew, for example, that the class was studying Greece and that there was a science fair project due the next week. The children of the more attentive parents were the ones who were doing better in class. Paying attention is such an important way of showing our children that we care about them and what happens to them. And it's not just the big things that count. Those toothless grins, the slide into second base, the homemade valentine: these are the little things that mean so much. Don't let them slip by unnoticed.

Directions: Talk with your children. Make it a point to have conversations with each of your children every day. Ask open-ended questions. Be available to talk. Get in the habit of talking openly and honestly so that they'll feel comfortable coming to you at any time.

Affection

A gallant child . . . makes old hearts fresh.
— William Shakespeare, *The Winter's Tale*

Each of my boys went through a really cute stage at about five years old where they said they wanted to marry me. This was their way of expressing affection for their mother, and it warmed my heart. Girls are really good at showing affection, maybe because women are by nature nurturers. My nieces give the best hugs!

Children have fewer inhibitions than adults do. They're more likely to show affection without fear of rejection. The trouble is, we don't always accept our children's love with open arms. We need to express affection for our children in every way possible. We need to tell them we love them, hug them, play with them, and comfort them. We each need to find ways to show our love for our children that are natural and comfortable for us and for our kids. We must never hesitate to show love; we must never withhold love as punishment. We can't turn it on and off like a faucet. Our kids need to know that they are loved at all times, not just when they're being "good."

Directions: Think up novel ways to express love. Leave a love note on the bathroom mirror, or on the pillowcase. Put a note or little candy hearts in today's lunchbox. Spell out "I LOVE YOU" in Alpha-bits® cereal in the breakfast bowl. Massage your spouse's feet after work.

Magnetic Attractions: "I love you." Sometimes the best way is to keep it simple and direct.

Time

Is this the little girl I carried; is this the little boy at play? I don't remember growing older . . . when did they? When did she grow to be a beauty; when did he grow to be so tall? Wasn't it yesterday when they were small? Sunrise, sunset, sunrise, sunset . . . quickly flow the days.

– Fiddler on the Roof

Time goes quickly, as we quickly find out when we have kids. They outgrow their shoes before they have a chance to wear them out!

I make it a point to arrange "dates" with each of my boys. Sometimes we just go to lunch or see a movie; sometimes we hang out at the mall. The important thing is that we spend time alone together. This is when we have our really good talks and get to know each other.

Every night I make sure that I have some quiet alone time with each child. We say prayers and I tell them how much I love them. John also takes his turn with them. He makes sure they're tucked in and comfortable and that they feel safe and loved. When the boys were younger, we would read to them every night. They both love reading now and read all kinds of books all the time.

What I like best in the whole world is Me and Piglet going to see you saying 'What about a little something?' and Me saying, 'Well, I shouldn't mind a little something, should you, Piglet,' and it being a hummy sort of day outside and birds singing.' 'I like that too,' said Christopher Robin, 'but what I like doing best is Nothing. It means just going along, listening to all the things you can't hear, and not bothering.'
— A. A. Milne, *Winnie the Pooh*

Sure, there's "quality time," but I think quantity time is vital, too. We don't have to go to Disneyland or the Natural History museum to spend time with our children. We can just be in the same room with them and feel their presence.

Magnetic Attractions: "We give each other attention, affection, and time." This message can be a reminder, or a discussion-starter. How can we better give each other attention, affection, and time?

Directions: The lost art of conversation! For one evening, pretend that the electricity has gone out. Gather everyone together in the living room or family room, turn off all the lights, make a fire in the fireplace (if you have one), and light some candles. On a warm summer night, you might want to sit outside with flashlights! Take turns telling stories. They can be stories that really happened, or you can make them up. You can even make it a game: tell a story and then have everyone guess if it really happened or not.

Beauty

The ocean floor looked wider than he had remembered, but Hermit Crab wasn't afraid. Soon he spied the perfect house – a big, empty shell. It looked, well, a little plain, but . . .
> – Eric Carle, *A House for Hermit Crab*

Because we feel a sense of belonging, our homes are the most beautiful places in the world to each of us. And our "home" is more than just the place where we live, the whole world is our home.

The house, the stars, the desert – what gives them their beauty is something that is invisible!
> – Antoine de Saint-Exupery, *The Little Prince*

How often do we look up and notice the beautiful clouds in the sky and all the shapes and figures they make so effortlessly? We tend to look past beauty, to look through it. If we take the time to stop and admire the flower, take in its fragrance, feel its soft petals, we let beauty into our lives. And appreciating the beauty in the world makes the journey that much richer.

People see God every day. They just don't recognize him.

– Pearl Bailey

People are beautiful! Beauty radiates from the light within. When we notice this light it actually shines brighter, and shines on us, creating warmth and love.

Humor is beautiful! Finding the humor in a situation is finding the beauty in that situation. It takes a keen eye sometimes, but it's always there. Laughter makes us more beautiful. We look better when we're smiling, and we're healthier people when we make humor a part of our lives.

Music is beautiful! It is amazing to think that music written by Bach, Mozart, and Beethoven, and so many others, so many years ago, has stood the test of time. It lasts because it expresses beauty in a way that words or pictures can't. Music stirs the emotions, it lets us feel. Listening to music is one experience, and creating music takes that experience to a whole different level. Music is the universal language. The notes are the same all over the world. It is a remarkable way to communicate.

When we are aware of beauty, in any expression, we are aware of God.

Directions: Notice what's beautiful. Take a Saturday morning walk. Take turns pointing out things that each person thinks are beautiful and have them explain why. Talk about it. One person may see a snake as beautiful while another says "Yuck!" Encourage the kids to talk about what's beautiful to them: the colors on the snake, the pattern, and the shape. Like the song says: "Everything is beautiful in its own way."

Magnetic Attractions: **"Be aware of beauty."** Sometimes all it takes is a gentle reminder. Point out beauty in each other to each other.

Play some of your favorite songs for your children. Let them play some of their favorite songs for you. Have a family concert. Give everyone an instrument and make your own music! No instruments? Try a percussion concert, find different "drums" around the house and see what sounds you can come up with. Strive for harmony!

Connection

I like the silent church before the service begins better than any preaching.

– Ralph Waldo Emerson

If you start with the "us" in your life and study up on the folks in your family, chances are you'll be an expert on how to get along in the big, wide world when you grow up.

            – Marlo Thomas, "Free to be . . . a Family."

It would appear that we are all totally separate individuals. But the truth is, we are all connected and what affects one person affects all. It may be difficult to grasp the idea that you're connected to someone you've never met on the other side of the world, but you can start with the idea of being connected to your own family.

The whole world is my family.

            – Pope John XXIII

Our heart is the sanctuary where the Lord of the universe . . . dwells in all His glory.

            – Swami Ramdas

Think about what it was like to be a new mom or dad. How often did you wake up in the middle of the night just before the baby started crying? We seem to have a sixth sense: we know when our children need us, we anticipate their calls. Developing this sense of connection is one of the things that makes us families.

My sister, Marci, and I have a deep connection. When we were living in different parts of the state and planning our weddings, we both registered for the same china pattern without knowing it. We bought the same coffee table for our living rooms! Our parents are amazed that they often receive the same birthday cards in the mail from each of us. It's not just that we have similar tastes, I know when she is going to call. She knows when I'm feeling down. We are connected because we are family, but we are spiritually in sync with each other as well.

Now join your hands, and with your hands your hearts.

– William Shakespeare

Directions: Get connected. The purpose of this exercise is to feel the energy of your connection. Just like electricity runs through wires, energy runs through our bodies, and we can use this energy to light up our lives and to show us the way! Have the family sit in a circle and hold hands. Tell everyone to close their eyes and breathe. (There may be some giggling if this is a new thing, just let it pass and everyone will settle down.) Select one person to start. Have him or her say one word that he or she wants to share with everyone. For example: Love, Peace, Joy, Faith, Gratitude. Then go clockwise around the circle and have everyone repeat what the person has said. Then have the next person do the same thing, saying a word and having everyone repeat it, and so on, until everyone has had a turn. You'll feel the energy and the connection. At the end, spend some time sitting in silence, then finish with a round of applause!

Travelers always look forward to coming home. Even after a great vacation, doesn't it always feel good to sleep in your own bed when you get home? A home filled with love is the best place to be. Home is where the family can congregate and be together.

3

All Aboard

> *It is a magnificent feeling to recognize the unity of complex phenomena, which appear to be things quite apart from the direct, visible truth.*
>
> – Albert Einstein

God is everywhere, in each one of us. This connects us all spiritually. We are all ONE.

We may seem to be separated by oceans, but we all live on ONE planet. We all walk on this same earth. We all feel the warmth of the same sun. We're all made out of the same molecules and "stuff" that everyone else is. It's just put together in a different combination. And thank God for our diversity! Imagine what a boring world this would be if we all looked and acted and thought the same way.

This connection isn't always so easy to see. When you're on the beach, you can look out at the ocean and see nothing but water for miles and miles, and then beyond the water, it looks like there is only sky. But we know that there is land further away. Just because we can't see it doesn't mean it isn't there.

We can't actually see the earth orbiting the sun, but we know it does. We see the sun in the daytime and not at night, but we know that morning comes, it never fails. We see God in expression every-where, every day. We're in this together. All aboard!

> *The trouble is that not enough people have come together with the firm determination to live the things that they say they believe.*
>
> – Eleanor Roosevelt

In a family, we feel a sense of togetherness all the time. We're all in the same boat! We live under the same roof, at least for a little while. We are individuals, but as a family we are a unit, we are ONE.

Directions: The next time you make cookies, invite your children to join you. Talk about how Oneness comes into play in the blending of ingredients to make the cookies. Organize all the ingredients separately: Eggs, butter, flour, sugar, whatever the recipe calls for. What do they all have in common? This recipe! Mix them together according to the directions. You can't tell where the eggs leave off and the butter begins. You can't separate the flour out. It's all a part of the whole. Now scoop the dough out by spoonfuls onto the cookie sheet. In every scoop of cookie dough, there is each of the ingredients. It is all ONE. The same cookie dough that was in the mixing bowl is contained in every cookie. The whole is contained in every part. Bake and enjoy. All of the cookies are different, different shapes and sizes, and yet they're all the same. This is interconnection at its finest. Discuss how this relates to your family, your community, and the Oneness of all things!

 Magnetic Attractions: "We are all ONE." That's what we are when we're connected, with our family and the outside world. Build a message from the books so far. "Our hearts are open. Tune in. We are all ONE."

Diversity

We're all on a path to get There. Even though our paths may be different, they all lead to the same place. We need to allow others to find their own way. No one way is better than another. We each make our own choices and we have an unlimited number of options available to us at anytime. Each choice is valid. Every person is important.

> Everybody is unique. Compare not yourself with anybody else lest you spoil God's curriculum.
>
> – *Baal Shem Tov*

We all live with the objective of being happy; our lives are all different . . . and yet the same.
– Anne Frank

When I took German in high school, our teacher matched us up with an English class in Germany. We were to write to our counterparts in German and then they would write back to us in English. I made friends with a girl named Karin from Stuttgart. She was my age and we had lots to talk about because we wrote each other back and forth constantly. We'd send photos and little gifts; it was a wonderful experience to communicate with someone so far away. I was impressed with how similar her life was to mine, with school, piano lessons, her pets, and friends. Although we lost touch long ago, I often think about her and wonder what she's doing now.

What this experience brought home to me is that all human beings experience the same basic emotions. We want to be loved – we want the freedom to express ourselves. We go about this in our own individual ways, but we have these things in common.

There is a lot of talk about "tolerance" right now, especially in our schools. While I understand that the intent to promote peace is there, I'm not crazy about the word "tolerance." To me that infers that there is something that must be tolerated, something that is somehow objectionable. I prefer to use the word "acceptance." I think we can embrace our diversity rather than merely tolerate it. And we can learn and grow from a diverse population that represents different races, religions, abilities, and cultures.

Directions: Travel to distant lands without leaving home! Help your children find pen pals. Or find one for yourself. Many schools have programs where the students write to other students in foreign countries. Check with your library to find out the addresses of some organizations for overseas pen pals. Or work with your children's school to set up a program in the classroom.

Magnetic Attractions: **"Every person is remarkable."** Name the ways that this applies in your family. "There is room here for everyone." Talk about what that means over dinner.

Acceptance

If you judge people you have no time to love them.

– Mother Teresa

It's easy to forget this basic human connection. Our world is filled with comparisons, with judgments: "I'm better than you are," "We don't have as much as they do," etc. Judgments are hurtful. Everyone's gain is someone's loss. Even if we come out on top, someone has to lose. And face it, there's always someone else around to usurp our status as the "best." Forget it. There's no point in comparing. There's room here for everyone.

An old Sufi story tells of two men who went before a judge to settle an argument. The judge listened to the first man and said, "You're right." Then the second man told his side of the story and the judge said, "You're right." The clerk stood up and said," Wait a minute! They can't both be right!" And the judge said, "That's right."

If your happiness depends on what somebody else says
(or does),then I guess you do have a problem.

– Richard Bach

What you think of yourself is much more important
than what others think of you.

– Seneca

We all want our children to have a healthy self-esteem, but this is not something we can "give" them, like we give them a gift. We can help them develop their self-esteem by how we speak to them, how we react to them. We need to show our children that we value them as people. And that we appreciate their efforts. Make it a given that they are loved and that they are perfect expressions of God. When giving praise or discipline, separate the behaviors from the individual doing them. Rather than saying: "You are a bad boy," say: "That was a bad thing to do!"

We want our children to know that they are inherently good no matter what they do, even when they do bad things. When they come home with an "A" on a test, rather than saying: "You are the smartest girl in the world," try saying: "You studied hard and it paid off, I'm proud of all the work you did." Praising a child's efforts helps motivate him or her to continue making the effort.

Do not worry about what others are doing! Each of us should turn the searchlight inward and purify his or her own heart as much as possible.

– Gandhi

As adults, we face criticism on a regular basis. But we have learned not to take that criticism personally. We understand the difference between criticism and judgment. When we're on the spiritual path, we practice nonjudgment. We know that we are all connected to God, and that there is no purpose in judging anyone or anything. We answer only to our own judgment of our own behavior.

> I'm kind to my friends, and kind to me, too, Because I'm important and so are you.
>
> *– Diane Loomans,* The Lovables in the Kingdom of Self-Esteem

We have to teach our children that the only thing that matters is what they know to be right or good, and that's between them and God. Teach them how important it is to just go about their business regardless of what people say, positive or negative. If they stop and listen to what everyone has to say, and give weight to it, they'll be on a roller-coaster of emotions. If they stand firm in their own convictions, they'll be fine. Model this behavior for them.

Directions: Play movie reviewer. See a movie with your children and ask them to write up a review. You can even have them just rate the movie on a scale of 1–10 (with 10 being the best) and ask why they gave the movie that rating. Then read some reviews of that same movie from different magazines and newspapers. They'll see that everyone has different opinions, and that their opinion is just as valid as the others. Talk about how the movie makers can't please everyone, but can only make the best movie from their own perspective. How would you make the movie differently?

Divine Perfection

If you are standing upright, don't worry if your shadow is crooked.

– Chinese Proverb

We are all perfect, just as we are. A story from India illustrates this point. A water bearer had two large pots, each hanging from opposite ends of a pole which he carried across his neck. One pot had a crack in it; the other pot was perfect and always delivered a full portion of water after the long walk from the stream to the master's house. The cracked pot always arrived only half full. Every day for two years, the water bearer delivered only one and a half pots of water to his master's house. Of course, the perfect pot was proud of its accomplishments. But the poor cracked pot was ashamed of its imperfection, miserable that it was able to accomplish only half of what it had been made to do.

After two years of what it perceived to be a bitter failure, the cracked pot spoke to the water bearer: "I am ashamed of myself, and I want to apologize to you." "Why?" asked the water bearer,

"What are you ashamed of?" "For these past two years, I have been able to deliver only half my load because the crack in my side causes water to leak out all the way back to your master's house. Because of my flaws, you have to do all of this work, and you don't get full value for your efforts," the pot said.

The water bearer felt sorry for the old cracked pot, and in his compassion he said, "As we return to the master's house, I want you to notice the beautiful flowers along the path."

As they went up the hill, the pot took notice of the sun warming the beautiful wild flowers on the side of the path, and this cheered it up some. But at the end of the trail, it still felt bad because once again, he had leaked out half of its load. The pot apologized again to the water bearer for its failure.

The water bearer said to the pot, "Did you notice that there were flowers only on your side of the path, but not on the other pot's side? That is because I have always known about your flaw, and I took advantage of it. I planted flower seeds on your side of the path, and every day while we walk back from the stream, you have watered them. For two years I have been able to pick these beautiful flowers to decorate my master's table. Without you being just the way you are, he would not have had this beauty to grace his home."

What we see as our flaws are really the little imperfections that make us unique and individual. We all have something to contribute. God doesn't make mistakes. Our "imperfections" make us perfect!

Directions: Get the whole family in on this one. Agree to spend an entire day being accepting and nonjudgmental. Get everyone to agree to consider everyone else's points of view. No one will jump to conclusions. Everyone will look for the perfection amid the imperfections. After dinner, compare notes on the day. How did you look at things differently? How did you feel about things? About yourself? Could you continue this for another day? And another?

Kindness

In the end only kindness matters. . . . We are God's hands.

– Jewel Kilcher

Magnetic Attractions: "Kindness matters." Talk about how and why. How do we feel when others are kind to us? When we're kind to others? It's one thing to be accepting of each other and ourselves. Now let's take it to another level and be kind to one another. Being kind honors the spirit within each of us. It is recognizing our connection as part of a spiritual family. And because we are all ONE, being kind to one of us is being kind to all of us.

What do we really notice about each other? Unless someone is wearing something totally outlandish, we don't really pay attention to his or her clothes. We don't always remember a hairstyle or an eye color. But we do notice if someone is nice to us or not. We notice kindness because we value kindness. Everything we say and do makes an impression. Be kind. Teach your children to be kind. Kindness matters.

Be kind, for everyone you meet is fighting a hard battle.

– Plato

We need to be sensitive to the fact that everyone carries burdens. All the more reason to be kind to everyone, even to people who are not kind to us. It is so important to remember that a lot of times we have no idea what's going on in another person's life. Someone who is not acting kindly may have had something terrible happen to him or her, and your kindness will help him or her feel better, and maybe that person will treat the next person he or she comes across with more kindness.

One day Brian came home from school a little down because he said his friend had been mean to him. But my kind and sensitive little guy didn't let it get to him. He said that he knew that his friend didn't mean it. He told me that his friend had gotten a pretty bad haircut the day before and was probably just in a bad mood.

 Directions: Do something kind for someone in your family today. Think of things you can do to show that person how much you care. Here are some ideas: Bring in the newspaper for Dad in the morning. Smile a lot. Give a heartfelt compliment. Help with the dishes. Take the dog for an extra long walk. Make brownies for dessert. Notice and comment when others are doing kind or helpful things too.

41

Keep a good tongue in your head.

— William Shakespeare, *The Tempest*

Kindness is not just what we say but also how we say it. Courtesy and good manners matter. We need to be polite and show respect for one another.

There is an old Middle Eastern poem that gives some good advice about this. It's called "Three Gates," and it basically says that before you speak, or "gossip," ask yourself these three questions: 1) Is it true? 2) Is it needful? 3) Is it kind? If you can honestly answer "yes" to these questions, then you may proceed. Otherwise, keep it to yourself!

'Let's go and see everybody,' said Pooh. 'Because when you've been walking in the wind for miles, and suddenly go into somebody's house, and he says 'Hallo Pooh, you're just in time for a little smackerel of something,' and you are, then it's what I call a Friendly Day.'

— A. A. Milne, *Winnie the Pooh*

Before I had children I taught at a modeling school and was assigned to teach the class called "Social Graces." I was amazed at how many of the teenage girls there did not know how to set a table! We are becoming more and more relaxed in this society, dressing more casually at work and so forth. But manners and courtesy serve a purpose far greater than mere formality. They help keep a certain order and dignity, they are ways of showing respect for one other.

Directions: Choose one day this week to set a formal table with the children. Go all out with candles and a centerpiece. It doesn't matter what food you serve, it could be macaroni and cheese! The purpose is the presentation! Set a beautiful table and set a good example.

Magnetic Attractions: "Set a good example." If you have a magnetic board, make it say "Set a good example." Use it for a centerpiece and a conversation starter at dinner. (Note: If you don't have a magnetic board, you can place the words in the middle of the table.)

'Don't grunt,' said Alice; 'that's not at all a proper way of expressing yourself.'

–Lewis Carroll, *Alice's Adventures in Wonderland*

When we choose our words carefully, and teach our children to do the same, we spread kindness. Words are powerful. They can demean and hurt, or they can soothe, heal, comfort, solve, praise, and honor. We are the best role models for our children. We can teach them to use words with dignity, not to demean people, not to be vulgar.

Directions: Next time the family goes to a restaurant, hold a little contest: see who can use the best table manners and speak the most politely. I started playing a little game with my boys to make them think about their manners every time they sit down. I pose multiple choice questions like these: When you're eating dinner, your napkin is placed: A) On your lap, B) On your head, or C) Under your plate. When you burp during dinner, you politely say: A) Excuse me, B) Thank you, or C) That was a good one. Now that they're getting the hang of it they're making up some funny ones of their own!

Action

Live truth instead of professing it.

– Elbert Hubbard

We must not, in trying to think about how we can make a big difference, ignore the small daily differences we can make which, over time, add up to big differences that we often cannot foresee.

– Marion Wright Edelman

Actions speak louder than words. We can say something a million times, but when we actually take action, it becomes the truth. It does no good to say one thing and do another. What is a person who's watching you going to believe? Walk your talk. Remember that your children are aware of what you are doing and are learning from your example.

Take Risks

Life is a great big canvas; throw all the paint on it you can.

– Danny Kaye

We can't play it safe all the time, sometimes it's best to just take the risk and take action. Teach your children that it's okay to fail. Explain to them that there really is no such thing as "failure" because by making an attempt they are getting one step closer to their goal. If they "fail" encourage them to try again. No matter how many times they fail, remind them that they are perfect – and loved – just as they are. Teach them to follow their hearts. Support that effort. If they keep trying, they will eventually succeed, and have plenty of people around to celebrate with!

Last year Brian's basketball team lost every single game they played. That can be hard for these little guys, to keep going out there game after game only to face defeat one more time. But our coach had a good attitude and made it really fun for the children. He encouraged them to keep trying, and to have fun with it. The team got to be a tight-knit group at the end of the season. They succeeded because they learned a lot about basketball and made new friends. And at our team party we all ate pizza and had a good time. It's all the same pizza, win or lose!

Magnetic Attractions: **"Go for it!"** On days when one of your children has a game or a math test, or you or your spouse have a tough day ahead at work, post the "Go for it!" message.

Feel Your Connection with Nature

No one shows a child the sky.

– African proverb

Children instinctively feel their connection to nature. Children aren't afraid of anything until they are taught to be afraid. We had a birthday party for Brian when he turned four years old. Brian loves animals, so we hired a company to bring live reptiles and put on a presentation for the children. The children just loved it! They petted the snakes and passed them around carefully. They held the iguanas and geckos and looked right in their eyes.

Most of the parents who were there made faces and wouldn't get near the animals. The telling moment came when the presenter brought out this HUGE python. It must have been ten feet long and as wide around as my leg. Every child draped that big snake over his or her shoulders and smiled! We got a photo of each of them to give away as party favors. The parents were not so brave. But, I have to admit, I learned something from those children. Under other circumstances I probably would have backed off and not held the snake. But after seeing what a great time the children were having being close to this incredible creature, I decided to go for it. I held out my arms and the snake was placed over my shoulders. He (or she, I'm not sure which) was heavy, and smooth. I could feel its strength, and out of courtesy, I thanked it for allowing me to hold it. Some of the other moms looked at me like I was crazy, but I was actually having fun. The snake and I posed for the camera and I got my photo taken, too!

My soul can find no staircase to Heaven unless it be through Earth's loveliness.

            – Michelangelo

Miracles are all around us and so easy and pleasant to discover in nature. Things grow and thrive side by side effortlessly. It all works the way it is supposed to.

We really are connected to every living thing. We eat the food that grows from the earth, we digest it, and it is a part of us. We breathe in oxygen and it is a part of our body. The plants that grow provide oxygen for us. By taking care of our planet, we are taking care of ourselves.

My mom is one of those "green thumbed" gardeners. Everything she touches grows and flourishes. When Freddy was little she taught him how to plant a vegetable garden. We had an abundance of tomatoes that summer! Freddy just loved taking care of his little plants, and watching them grow to produce all kind of good things that the whole family could share. He was especially proud when we'd eat his tomatoes with our dinner. By gardening, children can feel their connection with the earth. And by sharing the food that they grow, they feel their connection with the family.

Directions: This Saturday morning, take the children on a nature walk! Find nature wherever it is in your neighborhood. Walk through the park and look for signs of spring, or whatever season is headed your way. Lie on your back and find animals in the clouds. Find a pinecone and bring it home to make a bird feeder. Spread some peanut butter on it and roll it in birdseed (children love this part!). Hang it up outside your kitchen window and welcome the company!

Animals

'Not like cats!' cried the Mouse, in a shrill, passionate voice. 'Would you like cats if you were me?'
— Lewis Carroll, *Alice's Adventures in Wonderland*

Ferdinand ran to the middle of the ring and everyone shouted and clapped because they thought he was going to fight fiercely and butt and snort and stick his horns around. But not Ferdinand. When he got to the middle of the ring he saw the flowers in all the lovely ladies' hair and he just sat quietly and smelled.
— Munro Leaf, *The Story of Ferdinand*

We share this planet with each other, and also with our animal friends. We can learn a lot from these wonderful creatures. Look at Ferdinand the Bull. This was my favorite children's story when I was growing up. Maybe because I'm a Taurus, but also because I could relate to Ferdinand. He just wanted to do what he wanted to do. He wasn't concerned about living up to anyone's expectations, he just wanted to be happy; he just wanted to be himself and not hurt anyone. How could you not love a guy like that?

All I need to know I learned from my cat.

– Suzy Becker

Animals are true to their nature. They don't know how to lie. They live in the moment. They don't hide their feelings. They follow their instincts. They love unconditionally. That's pretty smart, don't you think?

Directions: Pay special attention to your pet. Bring him or her an extra treat. Let him or her out of her cage. Take your dog to the beach. If you don't have a pet, bring your children to the local animal shelter and adopt one. There are some wonderful animals that need good homes where they can be loved and appreciated. Be a responsible pet owner. Don't buy or breed animals (there are already plenty of pets to go around!) Make sure to have your pet spayed or neutered.

This is one planet that we all share. We're a diverse population of people – animals and plants – all living and growing together. We are intricately connected to God and to each other. When we treat each other with acceptance, kindness, and love, we are being true to our nature. We can be a peaceful planet. And we can start right now, by loving ourselves and our families, and letting that love spread out into the universe!

4

In for the Long Haul

'God is all that we dream of, and all that we seek,' said Old Turtle, 'all that we come from and all that we can find. God IS.'

– Douglas Wood, *Old Turtle*

Every child comes with the message that God is not yet discouraged of man.

– Rabindranath Tagore

Being in a family gives us a lot of perspective on the past, present, and future. We see the influence and the effects that past generations have had on our lives. We make decisions now that will affect our children's future. Given the broad view, we have an eternity to live, and yet not one minute to waste. That is, although our spirit is eternal, this one scenario we're living right now is fleeting. So we need to use our time wisely. Every moment is important.

There is no such thing as time, there is only now. Time is a linear measurement. It's a man-made invention. Who decided how long a second should be, or a minute, or an hour? We can only live in this moment in time. The past is done, the future hasn't happened yet. When we live in the present moment, we are aware of our presence, we are aware of our Selves!

We don't need to take a watch or even a stopwatch on this journey. It isn't a race! We all go at our own pace and get there when we get There. There are no deadlines to meet.

Timelessness

We don't remember days, we remember moments.

– Cesare Pavese

No day can be so sacred but that the laugh of a little child will make it holier still.

– Robert G. Ingersoll

On our way There, there will always be certain moments that we can look back on as having made a difference in our lives. I couldn't go back and tell you the dates when Freddy first giggled or Brian hugged his big brother. But I remember those moments vividly. I think we put too much emphasis on holidays as being the big days to show our love and spend time together. What about all the other days? Every day can be a holy-day! Holiness happens in the moment, not because of the calendar. We don't need presents, we just need presence! Show up wholly: body, mind, and spirit!

Directions: Find something to celebrate every day: a loose tooth, a new friend, or a completed business trip. Pretty soon you'll discover that you don't need an occasion to celebrate, you can just celebrate life!

Magnetic Attractions: "Today we celebrate: _____ _____." Use this message frequently both to announce reasons to celebrate and to remind your family to celebrate.

No one knows the story of tomorrow's dawn.

– African proverb

In our culture we're so geared toward the future: saving, planning, and worrying. But we can never know for sure what the future holds for us, so it doesn't do us any good to live in the future. We are here now and need to live here and now. If we're always looking ahead then we miss all the beauty of where we are! Of course we'll continue to plan for the future, but we have to be flexible in our planning, knowing that changes will inevitably have to be made depending on what happens between now and then.

Magnetic Attractions: "Every moment is important." It's important to remember this. Things happen in a family all the time that you just can't predict or plan for. These are just bumps in the road; some are little ones, and some are bigger ones. I never thought that my two boys would come down with the chicken pox when I had planned a weekend getaway. I never expected to have to find a private school for Freddy. But it does no good to try to fight these things. It's better to just go with the flow, live in the now, and do the best we can with what we've got. In a family, we're in it for the long haul.

'But Eeyore,' said Pooh, 'was it a Joke or an Accident?
I mean . . .'
 'I didn't stop to ask, Pooh. Even at the very bottom of the river I didn't stop to say to myself, 'Is this a Hearty Joke, or the Merest Accident?' I just floated to the surface and said to myself, 'It's wet.'
If you know what I mean.'
– A. A. Milne, *Winnie the Pooh*

Eeyore has the right idea. Why stress about it? What difference does it make? He's present to the moment. He's observing himself in his situation. He's paying attention and living in the moment. We can take a hint from Eeyore and be present in the moment. The next time you feel yourself stressing out about the future, bring yourself back to the now. Get out of your head, look around and use your sense of sight, smell, and touch to appreciate where you are at this moment.

Stay present. You'll always have time to worry later on if you want to.

– Dan Millman

If you're living presently, then later on, you won't be worrying either, because you'll be living in that moment!

 Directions: Call a "rest stop" day. Have the entire family go a day without wearing a watch or looking at a clock. You can even make a game out of discovering and covering up all the clocks in the house. There are so many of them now – the stove, the microwave, the computer, the television, the VCR, etc., etc., etc. Stay away from the television and radio which could give away the time (and take away the time!). Just live in the moment. Eat when you're hungry, sleep when you're tired. Enjoy the day.

 Magnetic Attractions: "Be present."
"Be present" is another timely reminder.

Commitment

*There is no commitment in the world like having children.
Even though they often will drive you to consider
commitment of another kind, the value of family still cannot
be measured.*

– Bill Cosby

When we marry, we make a commitment to our spouse. When we have children, our commitment is not only to them, but to the world, that we will raise these young people to be contributing, participating citizens of the world. What we get from this experience is immeasurable. Children open up the world to us in ways we never could have imagined.

The connection we have with our children is forever. As children start their journey, we are there to guide them. It's important that we get them off to a good start. When they stray, they look to us for direction. We are the most important influence on our children's spiritual lives. Parenthood continues always, even, and sometimes especially, after the child has grown into an adult. That bond is There.

Forever is composed of nows.

– Emily Dickinson

We'll get There, we've just got to keep going. The bumps in the road might slow us down, but they can't stop us. Each moment, one by one, makes up eternity. Each, person, each family, each community, each nation, makes up our one world, our one universe. We can take this journey one step at a time and we will get There.

The little things? The little moments? They aren't little.

– Jon Kabat-Zinn

Children remember little things of all kinds. We can enrich the journey by making sure they remember all the positive little things rather than all the little negative ones. Give praise generously, give affection lavishly. Notice all the good things children do and let them know that you notice! You know what they say? God is in the details!

Directions: Make a commitment to yourself and your children to live life spiritually, to pay attention, and to stay present. Remind yourself: "I am a spiritual being living a human existence!"

Organization

If the stars should appear but one night every thousand years, how man would marvel and adore."

– Ralph Waldo Emerson

The stars seem to hang in the sky effortlessly. They appear scattered like glitter in the air. But when we look closely, we know that the same stars appear in the same place, night after night, forever! And what is holding them there? God, and God's organizing power. The stars make up a map in the sky that we can follow to get anywhere we want to go.

Order is present everywhere. The stars are just one example of this. But how often do we look up at the awesomeness of it all? It's such a miracle, right in front of us, every night a spectacular show. And it's free, for all of us to enjoy!

Where else can we find order? The planets revolve around the sun. The sun "comes up" in the morning. The seasons change in the same order every year, they don't get mixed up! A seed grows into a flower, which produces more seed. Look at where we've created order, also. At an intersection there are traffic lights so that cars take turns and don't collide into each other. Cereal boxes are all rectangular so that they fit side by side in a cupboard. These common experiences are all part of one grand plan that links all of us together, forever.

Directions: Have fun finding your own examples of order in your home and in the world. Games are just one example. We have rules to follow, who goes first, etc. so that we all understand how to play and no one gets confused. Bring order to your life and to your mind. Think clearly, prioritize. Remember to put spirituality first!

Magnetic Attractions: "Put spirituality first with _____." (love, care, compassion). Choose the words that apply to you and your family.

Lighten Your Load

When we think about the continuum of our existence, and how our spirit lives forever, we've got to think about what we take with us and what we leave behind. We take with us all the love, wisdom, and experience we accrue. We leave behind all the love we give . . . and all the "junk" we accumulate! We have a big problem with our landfills. Some of that stuff is going to stay there forever!

We can bring more order and organization to our lives by simplifying things for ourselves. For example, we can cut down on the junk mail that we have to sort through and also help the environment by writing to: Stop the Mail, P.O. Box 9008, Farmington, NY 11735-9008. Just send them a letter requesting that your name not be sold to mailing list companies. This one act alone can cut down your junk mail as much as 75 percent. Another way you can bring order and organization into your household is to cut down on "stuff." Go through closets and cupboards and give away the things you don't need and don't use. When you have a clean cupboard you can see what's in there and get more use out of what you decide to keep. This is true for the children's toys, too!

> *Own only what you can always carry with you: Know*
> *languages, know countries, know people. Let your memory*
> *be your travel bag.*
>
> – Alexander Solzhenitsyn

Sometimes all the "things" we have just slow us down. When I travel, I try to just bring a small carry-on so that I don't have to wait to check luggage and then wait to pick it up again. Plus, there's always the possibility that it would get lost. So I'd rather not worry about it and just take what I can carry. It's a lot simpler that way, and it forces me to be a lot more organized in my thinking and in my packing.

On our spiritual journey, it's very similar. Don't be too attached to anything, because it just takes your attention away from what is really important. We don't have to live a spartan existence to be spiritual. We can be prosperous, AND live spiritually as long as we stay focused on God and not let the property become our priority. In fact, when we live spiritually we know that we already ARE prosperous. What is really of value to us is what helps us to grow spiritually: our experiences and our relationships, and we carry those with us always.

 Directions: Pack your travel bag. On this spiritual journey, make a list of the things you carry with you that help you to get There. It could be the Bible or another spiritual book that you've read, the lessons that a special teacher taught you, some words of wisdom, your relationships with people who are important in your life, things you've learned. Know that you can take as many of these kinds of things with you as you need and the load never gets any heavier. In fact, as we grow spiritually, we can carry even more.

Success

*To laugh often and much; to win the respect of intelligent
people and the affection of children; to earn the appreciation
of honest critics and endure the betrayal of false friends; to
appreciate beauty, to find the best in others; to leave the
world a bit better, whether by a healthy child, a garden, or a
redeemed social condition; to know even one life has
breathed easier because you have lived. This is to have
succeeded.*

– Ralph Waldo Emerson

Too many people define success in terms of money. This is really
narrow-minded thinking. I like Emerson's definition the best.
This is the kind of success we want our children to strive for.
These are the kinds of signposts that point us in the right
direction on our journey.

Success often comes from not knowing your limitations.

– Frank Tyger

If you insist on seeing limitations, you make them real. There
are no limitations, there are only possibilities! See the possibilities and you'll be successful.

Directions: See with your mind's eye. It's easy for us to picture some place we've already been. Say we want to go to the mall. If we stand at our front door and look, we probably cannot see the mall with our eyes, but we can see it with our mind's eye. We know where it is and we know how to get There. Now picture someplace you want to be where you haven't yet been, and it doesn't have to be a place found on a map. For example, maybe you want to be the number one sales rep for your company, or maybe your child wants to be president of her class. See yourself there. What does it feel like? What are you doing? The more you picture yourself there, the more your mind will help you to find your way there.

Magnetic Attractions: "See the possibilities." Make "See the possibilities" your theme for the day or week. Post the message and start a list of possibilities for your family.

Only those who dare to fail greatly can ever achieve greatly.
– Robert F. Kennedy

Robert F. Kennedy is one example of someone who will live forever in the heart of our nation. Children learn about people like him who have achieved great success in their lives. Their stories live on.

Babe Ruth is one of the most famous baseball players who ever lived. He is best known for the 714 home runs that he hit. That is quite an impressive statistic. But did you know that the same Babe Ruth also struck out 1,330 times? Failing does not hurt a person. The only thing that can stop your success is if you fail to make the effort. You must always try. Babe Ruth knew this and kept stepping up to the plate. We can learn from his example and just keep going no matter what. That's what determination is all about.

Families face challenges every day. We have our troubles and our disagreements. But if we're determined to get through these things, we will. It's important to stick together and help each other when the going gets tough.

> My own experience has taught me this: if you wait for the perfect moment when all is safe and assured it may never arrive. Mountains will not be climbed, races won, or lasting happiness achieved.
>
> – Maurice Chevalier

Abraham Lincoln had great determination and persistence. His business failed, he went bankrupt, his fiancée died, and he had a nervous breakdown. Lincoln lost eight elections before he was elected President of the United States. Lincoln had great faith, and would often say of his setbacks, "It's a slip and not a fall."

We can be there to encourage each other and to remind each other of our true value. Sometimes when we feel like we've lost faith, we can borrow some from a family member.

Children face setbacks while on their journey, too. Maybe one doesn't get a part in the school play, or one doesn't make the hockey team. We can help them through this disappointment by reminding them that others have gone through the same experiences, and gone on to great success because they didn't give up.

Directions: Write a recipe for success that your family can follow. Here are some suggested ingredients: Patience, flexibility, persistence, kindness, faith.

Opportunities

You must live in the now and be wide awake to your opportunities.
— Florence Scovel Shinn

When children are given boundaries, they feel a sense of order in their lives. We all need that sense of order. Children crave routine and rituals. Every parent has experienced a favorite video being played ad infinitum! To children predictability equals stability. It makes them feel safe and confident. The best and easiest way to do this is to establish routines. It might sound boring, but routine helps to make our hectic lives simpler; it opens us up to the opportunities around us.

Now that my children are older and have a lot of homework each day, we are into the routine of doing homework right after school. They know that this is what is expected of them and that they cannot go on to their other activities until the homework is complete. We started this routine early on and it has worked out really well.

When Freddy was a newborn, bedtime wasn't a big deal. He always slept very well because we had a set routine. After Brian was born, his routine was upset, and it took him a while to get back in the swing of things. He didn't want to go to bed at night, partially I think, because he wanted to spend time alone with his mom and dad. We got him back into the bedtime habit by reading to him at night, or making up stories. I used this as an opportunity to talk to my little boy and learn more about him, and as an opportunity to teach him when I had his undivided attention.

> *On and on you will hike. And I know you'll hike far and face*
> *up to your problems whatever they are.*
> — Dr. Seuss, *Oh, The Places You'll Go*

Sometimes we defeat ourselves by the words we use. If we're careful in choosing our words, we can actually create possibilities in our lives. By thinking of our "problems" as "challenges," for instance, we turn obstacles into opportunities.

Magnetic Attractions: "Today is an opportunity to _____." If you don't have a magnet for your particular opportunity, write it on a slip of paper. In fact, every member of your family can write (or say if they're too little to write) their opportunity on a slip of paper. Post the slips using the "opportunity" magnet to hold them up.

There's always another way to say something. Use the most positive, empowering words when describing your children. For example, instead of calling a child a "daydreamer," say that he is imaginative and creative. Instead of calling him "impulsive," you could say that he is spontaneous. It might just be semantics, but it makes a big difference in how a child thinks about himself and how he is perceived in the world.

> *Bad times have scientific value. These are occasions a good*
> *learner would not miss.*
>
> > – Ralph Waldo Emerson

When times are not going as well for us as we'd like, we learn the most. Bad times are an opportunity to grow, to learn, and to get stronger. It's so important to be able to bounce back after failing. Try to find the unexpected opportunities in your setbacks. This is also such an important lesson for children. Be a family that doesn't give up when the going gets tough.

> *Remember – nothing will happen that you and God can't*
> *handle together.*
>
> > – Author unknown

Our faith in God will get us through anything and everything.

> *I thank God for my handicaps, for, through them, I have found*
> *myself, my work, and my God.*
>
> > – Helen Keller

Helen Keller is a perfect example of someone who learned and grew from all of her experiences as a handicapped person. She and her teacher, Anne Sullivan, opened up the whole world to handicapped people. Their work and writings still inspire and encourage people today.

Every family is going to have some challenges to face. When we first found out about Freddy's Attention Deficit Disorder (ADD),

I had no idea what we were dealing with. I had to educate myself about this condition, and find a team of professionals to help our family sort out all the information. It took a while to get on the right track, but I learned and grew from the experience, and I know everyone in our family did, too.

Magnetic Attractions: "Have faith." It's a simple message. We can't see it too often. Through a nonprofit organization and support group for parents, CH.A.D.D. (Children and Adults with Attention Deficit Disorders), I had the opportunity to meet other parents in our situation. Later I volunteered to help our local chapter and learned and grew from the experience of helping other parents as well. I knew that I wasn't alone, that other parents were going through the same kinds of things that John and I were. Those parents helped me and I saw how others could benefit from my suggestions and resources. When things change for the better, they are changed forever. We can't go backwards on this journey. People we help go on to help others; it's a continuing cycle of this spiritual world. When we see this, we know that we are offered many marvelous opportunities to grow and change together.

5

Finding Our Way

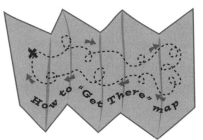

Trust yourself. You know more than you think you do.

– Benjamin Spock

We know all the answers to all the questions in the universe. We just don't know that we know them! Even if we get this intellectually, we don't know and accept it on a deep soul level or we would already be There! What we're actually learning on this journey, is what we already know.

That's why, each step of the way, we know we're in the right place, because it feels right. It feels familiar, like we've been there before, because we have! When you're driving somewhere with your children, ask them for directions. Point out that they know how to get there, because they've been there before. Freddy and Brian have never driven themselves to school, but they could show someone the way because they've gotten there hundreds of times before.

Awareness

I yam what I yam and that's all that I yam.

— Popeye, the Sailor Man

Bet you didn't know that Popeye was such a spiritual guy, huh? I am all that I am. Meditate on that. That little sentence is so true and so profound. Open up your awareness to encompass all that you truly are. Don't be defined by your title, the roles you play, or the hats you wear. Be aware of your true divinity. Practice saying: I am an expression of God.

There is nothing outside you. That is what you must ultimately learn.

— A Course in Miracles

Everything that we see is subject to our perception. We may see a tree, a frying pan, or a sweater. But what is really there is a combination of matter made up to look like those things. We're all made of the same "stuff." When you take away all the physical matter that composes our bodies, which is less than 1 percent of the total body, all that's real is love. We are 99 percent empty space! It's incredible to think of it this way, but it's a great way to illustrate how so much of what we believe to be real is actually an illusion.

Directions: Here's a fun exercise to do with your children that helps to illustrate this point and also makes another. Get a big glass jar, like a pickle or mayonnaise jar. Then gather up some rocks, stones, pebbles, and sand. Start with the biggest rocks first, and fill the jar. Is it full? Add some of the smaller rocks? Full yet? Add some of the smallest rocks . . . and then some of the sand. When you think the jar is really full, add water. There is a lot of empty space for the water to seep into. It is also important to notice that everything fits in the jar because you started with the biggest things first. If you filled the jar with sand and water first, the big rocks wouldn't fit. Life works that way, too. First, fill up your life with big things, like spirituality and family. Then there will still be plenty of room for the little things, like comic books or baseball cards, or whatever else is important to you.

Magnetic Attractions: "**Trust yourself.**" It's a good reminder to post whenever anyone in the family is faced with a challenging experience.

The gull sees farthest who flies highest.
    – Richard Bach, *Jonathan Livingston Seagull*

We can't see much down from the ground. When we rise above, we get a better view. We can rise above the pettiness and problems of a mundane life by committing to a spiritual life and by taking action to live and grow spiritually.

> *I am still learning.*
>
> – Michelangelo's motto

We are always learning, constantly, at every age and every stage. Even in our sleep we are learning through our dreams. Dream journals can help us to learn more about ourselves. I keep a notebook and pen by my bed and write down my dreams when I wake up at night. Sometimes I can't read my writing in the morning; sometimes I can read the writing but I can't make sense of the words! But when I can remember and figure out my scribbles, I look in my dream interpretation book to get some insight. It's always fascinating to look into what's going on at that subconscious level. And it builds awareness.

Magnetic Attractions: "We are always learning." Remind your family that means all of us – mom and dad, as well as children. Don't be afraid to learn new things as a family – whether it's assembling a bookcase or reading a spiritual book aloud.

Directions: Take an awareness test. Close your eyes. What clothes are you wearing? What did you eat for breakfast? What did you dream last night? Was it in color or black and white? Do this test as often as you like.

When we are aware, we are living in the moment. We pay attention to our clothes when we get dressed, we notice the feel of the fabric against our skin, the warmth and the comfort. We pay attention to our food and its flavor when we eat it. Our senses are heightened when we are aware, and they come into play to help us to remember even little details of our experiences. Even with your eyes closed, you can "see" yourself in your mind's eye. See yourself now as pure love and light.

Knowledge

Strange how much you've got to know before you know how little you know.

– Author unknown

We tend to learn in layers. We discover life at deeper and deeper levels. We can hear the same thing a dozen different times and understand it differently each time. Really good movies can be watched over and over again and we get something out of it each time. We see new things, things we may have missed the first or second time around but that now seem so obvious and clear. There's all this text and subtext in the script, we take note of the art direction and the significance of certain recurring themes, and the music now takes on greater meaning. Life is the same way. Our experiences are revealing more and more layers of the truth. We learn and grow as we go.

Have you ever noticed how children like to watch the same video over and over again? They like what they are familiar with. They feel smart knowing what is going to happen. The videos seem simple to us, but children learn from them on their level. They've got to master "Blue's Clues" before they can take on "Gone With the Wind."

No es lo mismo hablar de toros, que estar en el redondel.
It's not the same to talk of bulls, as to be in the bull ring.

– Spanish proverb

There's theory, and then there's practice. We could read books about spirituality all day long, but if we don't embody the principles in our own lives, what have we learned? The process needs to go from the head to the heart and back into the world. For example, we've read that meditation is good for us in many ways. We understand this to be true and wholeheartedly agree. But do we meditate daily? Do we make this practice a priority in our lives? Do we appreciate the benefits of meditation as we go about our day and interact with people? We can't get There by looking at a map, we've got to take the steps!

The more I learn the more I realize I don't know.

– Albert Einstein

Albert Einstein is considered to be one of the greatest geniuses of our time. He was a scientist, a philosopher, and a peacemaker and won the Nobel Prize for Physics in 1922. Yet this brilliant man was a very poor student. He was introverted and withdrawn and showed little scholastic ability. Einstein left school at the age of 15 with poor grades. When he first applied to the Polytechnic Institute in Zurich, he failed the entrance exam. His passion for knowledge could not be deterred. When Einstein became a success, he had much to teach his own students. He understood the struggles that school could present and often would write to students with encouragement and help them outside of class with homework. He learned beyond what books could teach, and used this knowledge to help others. Our own experiences growing up can help us relate to our children. I totally understand Freddy's difficulties with his ADD because I went through the same thing at his age. Brian likes to be on the stage. I can help him prepare for his performances because I've done plays myself. These are things you can't just read about to learn. You have to actually have the experiences, you have to have taken those turns!

Knowledge rests not upon truth alone, but upon error also.
                                                              – Carl Jung

We also learn through our mistakes. Let your children know that it's okay to make mistakes. Home should be a place where they can feel free to fail and know that they are loved regardless.

It's what you learn after you know it all that counts.
                                                              – John Wooden

We don't really know it all at the same time. Our brains are not wired for that; we would go crazy trying to sort out and find the information we needed. There's no purpose in carrying it all around with us all the time. But we can know that all of the information we need is but a thought away. We don't need to know everything, because whatever we don't know, we can find out. Information is ours to share. We can learn anything we choose to learn.

 Directions: Choose a topic you've always been curious about and write a report. Go about this as you would a seventh grade homework assignment. Ask a question, do the research, write down what you learn. Need help getting started? Here are some ideas: Do cats see color? (This was Freddy's science project this year and it was very interesting!) What kinds of plants are native to your area? What is the status of the world population growth? Who invented angel food cake? You'll be surprised at how much you can learn; the information is out there!

Wisdom

Wise men hear and see as little children do.

– Lao Tzu

It's that childlike curiosity that compels us to question. When we question, we learn; we gain insight into the mechanics of the world. Little children approach life with an open mind. They explore, they look with wonder and awe. What a wonderful way to approach the pursuit of knowledge. It makes us wise. Your children can teach you everything you need to know about remaining open to life.

The young man knows the rules but the old man knows the exceptions.

– Oliver Wendell Holmes

Age gives us the benefit of added experience. We have more time to take in knowledge and apply it to different areas in our lives. We take what we know and assimilate it with what we do. Knowledge well used becomes wisdom, a higher knowledge.

The years teach much which the days never know.

– Ralph Waldo Emerson

In Japan, September 15th is Respect for the Aged Day. That culture understands the value of their aging community. People who have lived many years have a lot of wisdom and experience, and we can learn from them. We need to show more respect for the elderly and to appreciate the lessons that they have to share with us.

 Directions: Spend time with grandparents or great-grandparents today. Or visit a senior center and volunteer your time. Bring a chessboard and play a game with someone there; you'll pick up some good moves! Bring a crochet hook and some yarn and you're sure to find someone to teach you how to make an afghan.

You know . . . everybody is ignorant, only on different subjects.

– Will Rogers

No question is stupid, no person is stupid. We all have our expertise, which means we all have our areas of ignorance, too! But if we work together, it all comes together. What I know helps someone, and what that person knows helps me. All together, we fill in all the blank spaces. Your knowledge contributes to the whole. Your participation makes a difference.

Magnetic Attractions: "Honor what you know." It's important to remember this. Post the message as a reminder and then take the time to appreciate each other's knowledge. In school, students who are struggling can be hooked up with other students who can help them in a certain area. And the help can be reciprocal. For example, one student is having trouble with math, but is a really good basketball player. Another student is great at math, but can't make a free throw shot and wants to improve. These two can be an asset to each other. It's a win-win situation.

In his book *Frames of Mind*, Howard Gardner outlines seven distinct types of intelligences:

Spatial Reasoning: The ability to understand how things relate in space. This is often indicated by a skill at building things, and an ability to visualize what something looks like from different sides.

Music: An instinctual attraction to sound.

Language: A love of language and the written word.

Math and Logic: Dominated by reasoning power. A penchant for math and science.

Interpersonal Intelligence: An ability to understand other people.

Intrapersonal Intelligence: Self-knowledge. This intelligence tends to deepen throughout life.

Movement: The capacity to use your whole body or parts of your body to solve problems or make things.

Directions: Explore your personal learning style. How do you best learn? Think about your children's learning styles. How can you encourage them in the ways they learn best?

Motivation

If you ask what is the good of education, the answer is easy – that education makes good men, and that good men act nobly.
— Plato

There is purpose to learning. It's not just accumulating facts. The benefit of education is connecting knowledge to the self, to grow from the experience. On our journey, we're not just looking at the odometer and putting miles on the car. We're taking in the sights, meeting people along the way. We're learning and we're growing.

> *And when you're in a Slump, you're not in for much fun.*
> *Unslumping yourself is not easily done.*
>
> – Dr. Seuss, *Oh, The Places You'll Go*

Everyone gets in a slump now and then. It's hard to keep accelerating, sometimes we have to coast for awhile. The important thing that Dr. Seuss is saying is that we have to "unslump" ourselves. No one can do it for us. Whether it's finding a novel idea or a new approach to a problem, it's up to us to do it.

> *Although we try hard to inspire our children to do good work*
> *on their own, the motivation for such work always has to*
> *come from inside them.*
>
> – Bill Cosby

One key to motivating children, and ourselves, is relevance. "How does this affect me? What does this mean to me? How is this important in my life?" If we can find a way to make a subject relevant from the child's perspective, we'll be much more successful in teaching that child. For example, Freddy's humanities class recently did a unit on feudal Japan. This didn't ring any bells for Freddy, he didn't see where he would ever use this information so he wasn't much interested. Then I reminded him about the Ninjas from that time period. He's been taking karate since he was four years old and he has an interest in things like that. He did a report on the weaponry used in that time, and ended up learning a lot about Japan in the process.

Directions: Make a list of ways you can "unslump" yourself. Keep this list handy for times when you do get in a slump, and can't think of anything to do to get out of it! Help your children "unslump," too.

Directions: Begin to earn your own wings by starting something you've been meaning to do for some time: quit smoking, strike out on a new career, or plant the first seed in next year's garden!

Creativity

But it is impossible that the creative power should exclude itself. Into every intelligence there is a door which is never closed, through which the creator passes.

– Ralph Waldo Emerson

When I was younger I could remember anything, whether it happened or not.

– Mark Twain

We are creative beings – that is our nature. We are creating all the time. We are expressing ourselves all the time.

Children make up stories and this is a way for them to express their creativity. We should encourage this! Ask: "And then what happened?!" instead of saying: "Come on, don't be silly." This story-telling is a kind of verbal "doodling." It's practice for mastering a skill.

Lots of children draw cartoons and figures in their notebooks, or in the margins of the paper when they're taking notes in school. Take a look at those drawings; some of them are pretty good! You just might have a budding artist on your hands . . . or I should say a real artist on your hands! I've learned there is a difference. My five-year-old niece, Grace, was still wearing her ballet costume when she went to get her hair cut. The stylist looked at her and said: "Oh, my! You're a budding ballerina!" Grace looked at her quizzically and said, "No, I'm a real ballerina!"

You might want to keep some musical instruments around the house. We've got a piano, a couple of guitars, some ukuleles, a recorder, harmonica, a kazoo . . . and lots of percussion instruments that make unusual sounds. Freddy and Brian take piano lessons because I want them to be able to read music. I took piano when I was young and know what an influence music has had on my life. I want my children to have the same love for music, and I know that they do! They practice the music that is assigned to them, but most of the time, they just "doodle" with the instruments. I think it's great to let them experiment and see what they can do. They may not want to be professional musicians, but all this activity helps to develop their creativity, which they'll use no matter what field they decide to go into.

Children should be encouraged to "doodle" in many different ways.

Man's mind, stretched to a new idea, never goes back to its original dimensions.

— Oliver Wendell Holmes, Jr.

Creativity and spirituality are one and the same. When we are being creative, we are being spiritual, we feel close to God. Time flies by. We are "in the flow." This causes us to grow, and we never grow "backwards." We don't shrink, we only grow some more!

So how can we encourage creativity? First, it's important not to overorganize our own or our children's schedules. Leave plenty of time for everyone to pursue their own interests, to play without being interrupted by appointments and commitments. Allow "doodling" in different media: language, drawing, clay, cooking, etc. Don't evaluate the work. Children should just be concerned with how they feel about their accomplishments. They shouldn't be worrying about how they will be judged or graded on their creative endeavors. Avoid competition when it comes to creativity. Different forms of creativity cannot be compared the way that sports can be scored. Give children space, allow them to be original and support their interests.

 Directions: Buy each person in your family a blank book that they can write in whenever they feel like it. The books with the unlined pages are best because you can also draw without lines getting in the way. You can also cut photos or words out of magazines, jot down ideas, or keep track of dreams. This is each person's book to fill up however they want to. They can be shared with the family or kept private.

Directions: Get out those boxes of old photos and arrange them in albums. Do one album by theme and others chronologically. Flip through the life you've created with your family so far.

Teachers

'Why,' said the Dodo, 'the best way to explain it is to do it.'
— Lewis Carroll, *Alice's Adventures in Wonderland*

There are those who depend on us, watch us, learn from us, take from us. And we never know. Don't sell yourself short. You may never have proof of your importance, but you are more important than you think.

— Robert Fulghum

What would you do differently if you knew that people were watching you? Imagine that you're a celebrity and you're being followed by journalists and fans. Would you toss trash on the ground? Would you swear? Would you burp without excusing yourself? Chances are, you'd be on your best behavior! Put yourself in that position for one day and see how differently you act. Pick up that stray piece of trash. Be kind and smile. Have good manners.

Children watch adults, and adults watch children, too! I know I'm always impressed with a kid who does something nice to help other people. It makes me want to do something nice, too. That's the way it works. And little children watch big children and want to be like them, so they follow their example. It's been this way always. Children are teachers, too.

Is not, indeed, every man a student, and do not all things exist for the student's behoof?

– Ralph Waldo Emerson

As teachers, what tools do we have to work with? The whole world is our classroom! It's all happening all around us every day.

 Directions: Who are the teachers in your life, and what have they taught you? Who do you think you teach, and what do you teach them? This list can change daily. Think about it every once in awhile.

We are finding our way every day on this journey. And we have resources at our disposal, we don't have to stumble around in the dark. People who have been There can help point us in the right direction. Books we read are a great source of information, people we meet, conversations we have, the examples that people set by the way they live their lives . . . these are all indicators we can use like a compass. We learn from experience, we learn from living, and we learn from sharing.

6

Room for Everyone

To us, family means putting your arms around each other and being there.

– Barbara Bush

When we are children, it seems like we have our parents all to ourselves for quite a long time. Our home and our family is our own little island, with everything we need or want. But when we do, inevitably, venture out into the world, for school and a social life, we learn that we don't live on an island at all. Our families are really part of one huge global family. As members of that family, we need to be considerate and responsible and we need to contribute; we need to share.

Communication

It is the privilege of adults to give advice. It is the privilege of the youth not to listen. Both avail themselves of their privileges, and the world rocks along.

– D. Sutten

Communication between parent and child takes place long before the child is even born. I could feel my babies kick and squirm and I could even feel when they had the hiccups! I could rub my big belly and soothe them. I felt that we could communicate without words, that I was sending them mental images of love.

When babies are born we cater to their every need. As they get older, they get frustrated and cranky when they cannot communicate those needs to us. Joseph Garcia has written a book called *Toddler Talk* that explains how we can teach sign language to very young children. Babies as young as eight months old can learn to sign. Children who use this language tend to be more calm and relaxed because they have a way to communicate with their parents that works! My friend, Katheryn, is using this technique with her daughter, Skylar, and having great results, and a lot of fun!

Remember, communication doesn't just happen when your children learn to talk. I have heard that for every one word that a child knows how to speak, he or she understands about 100 more words. Be careful what you say around your child! He or she is not only picking up on the words that you say, but the inflection in your voice and your body language. Say good, positive, loving, sweet things. Say prayers, give blessings, show gratitude.

To say these words is nothing. But to mean these words is everything.

— A Course in Miracles

Magnetic Attractions: "Let's talk." Post it after an argument, once the air has cleared some. Go on a walk and talk it out. Listen. Forgive.

Communication works both ways. Half of the equation is listening. We need to really listen to our children. We need to ask questions and let them know that we are available to them. Children don't communicate the same way that adults do. Instead of putting emphasis on their actual words, tune into their emotions. By acknowledging all their emotions, we communicate acceptance. Help children to understand that feelings aren't good or bad, they just are. Sometimes Brian says: "I don't want to talk about it," and yet he follows me around the house waiting for me to draw him out. I just reassure him that when he's ready, I'll listen. And I promise not to give advice unless he asks for it. That's usually enough to get him to say what is on his mind.

> I'll share your milk and your cookies, too -
> The hard part's sharing mine with you.
>
> —*Shel Silverstein*

Magnetic Attraction: "We are here for each other." Those things that seem like they go without saying often need to be said.

We also need to live up to our promises. When we say, "We'll get a cookie next time," then we'd better be prepared to make good on that promise because our child will surely remember!

It's okay to apologize to our children, too. A lot of parents don't like to admit that they are wrong, they feel that they are giving away their power, that their children will have the "upper hand." In fact, apologizing shows respect for our children, and our children will respect us for that in turn. It also sets a good example to our children that apologies are appropriate and that good can come as a result of an apology.

Our communication with our children goes beyond words. I recently heard a story about a single mother raising a teenage daughter. The daughter was constantly pushing her limits and was becoming increasingly rebellious. Just when it seemed that things couldn't get worse for these two, the daughter was arrested for drunk driving and her mother was called to pick her up. The next day at home they didn't talk at all. Finally, the mother broke the tension and gave her daughter a small gift-wrapped box. The daughter opened it reluctantly to find a small rock. She said: "Oh, great, Mom, is this some kind of a joke?" The mother handed the girl a card. When this bold teenager took it out of the envelope and read the message, tears streamed down her face. She gave her mother a big hug. On the card, her mother had written these words: "This rock is more than 200 million years old. That's how long it will take before I give up on you."

There are a lot of ways to communicate with your children. Freddy and Brian and I have a secret signal. When we're walking along I'll squeeze their hand three times. That means "I love you." Then they squeeze mine back twice. That means: "Me, too."

Directions: Invent your own secret signals for your family. Be creative! And pay attention so you get the signals when they're sent!

Giving

Give, and it will be given to you.

– Jesus

This is the natural law of the universe. Giving and receiving are the same thing. They are two sides of the same coin; you can't have one without the other.

A man there was and they called him mad; the more he gave the more he had.

– John Bunyan

Whatever you want more of in your life, give it away. If you want love, give love. If you want money, give money. If you want friends, give friendship. There is an unlimited supply and it is ours to tap into. Try it for yourself and you'll see how it works!

They who give have all things; they who withhold have nothing.

– Hindu proverb

'I'm very glad,' said Pooh happily, 'that I thought of giving you a Useful Pot to put things in.' 'I'm very glad,' said Piglet happily, 'that I thought of giving you something to put in a Useful Pot.' But Eeyore wasn't listening. He was taking the balloon out, and putting it back again, as happy as could be . . .

– A. A. Milne, *Winnie the Pooh*

Eeyore was so happy because he knew that Pooh and Piglet were not just giving him some silly presents, they were giving him love and attention. It meant a lot to him that these two friends were thinking of him. And it made Pooh and Piglet happy to see Eeyore so happy. When we give our love and attention we are sharing ourselves.

. . . man cannot earn anything, his blessings come as gifts. With the realization of wealth, we receive the gifts of wealth. With the realization of success, we receive the gifts of success, for success and abundance are states of mind.

– Florence Scovel Shinn

The more we share, the more we have.

– Leonard Nimoy

Everything we think we want, we really have already. We just need to know that it is ours! Everything we give away, is really everyone's anyway, so it's not like we're losing anything. What we give comes back to us. Giving leads to growth. Whatever we give, we have more of. If you want love, give love. Give a hug and you get one back! It's pretty amazing, really.

My family sees this happen every year at Christmas time. Before the holidays, we go through all the toys and give all that are outgrown or undesired to charity. We also shop for new things that we wrap and put under the tree at our church. These gifts are distributed to needy families in our area. Remarkably enough, all the space left vacant in the closets is filled again before New Year's!

 Directions: Organize a giving drive at your school or church. Have it be whatever is of interest to your group. You may want to hold a book drive to give books to underprivileged schools. Children can participate by distributing flyers, making announcements in class, and cleaning out their closets. You might want to collect canned foods for your local food bank. Whatever it is you decide on, do it up big, and watch the great response you get. Then see how good it feels to give it all away!

Service

The smallest good deed is better than the grandest good intention.

– Duguet

Service is a form of giving; it is giving of yourself. A lot of people intend to do good things, but never actually get around to it. Make service a regular part of your life.

Think about what you have to share with the world. I always think about "sharing" as that first block of time in elementary school where we could bring in things to "share" with the class. My children did this, also, and I was often surprised by the things that they chose to bring in. One day Freddy actually brought his little brother Brian in for show and tell! He hid Brian under his desk until it was time to share. Then Freddy raised his hand, and the class played "Twenty Questions" trying to figure out just what he'd brought to share. They finally gave up, and Brian popped up from under the table. Freddy shared his little brother with all of his friends!

 Directions: Make a list over dinner of what each of you can share with the world.

In June I saw a charming group of roses all begin to droop. I peeped them up with chicken soup! Sprinkle once sprinkle twice sprinkle chicken soup with rice.
  – Maurice Sendak, *Chicken Soup With Rice*

The way to be of service is not to think: "What am I going to get out of this?" but to think: "Where can I be of most help?" Service must be given without expectation of anything in return.

There are some beautiful giraffes at the Santa Barbara Zoo where my family has a membership. One thing we learned is that giraffes have a larger heart than other mammals in proportion to the rest of its size. Why is that? Because the giraffe has a long neck and it is always sticking its neck out. It needs a larger heart to keep its blood flowing. We can learn from these animals: The more we stick our necks out to help others, the bigger our hearts get!

 Directions: Where can you be of service today? Who needs help that you can give? Commit to doing some kind of service each week.

Empathy

. . . he is the only one of them all who does not seem to me ridiculous. Perhaps that is because he is thinking of something else besides himself.

— Antoine de Saint-Exupery, *The Little Prince*

Carlyle, son of a mason and grandson of a carpenter, showed his gifts early. At the age of eleven months he heard another child in the household crying and although he had never, before that, uttered a word he sat up and said, "What ails wee Jock?"

— Catherine M. Cox

Children are naturally full of empathy. They are sensitive to another child's cries. They know, they feel, they remember. We lose a lot of our empathy when we grow up and have to worry about ourselves and our own place in the world. But if we remember our connection to each other, empathy is not hard to find.

My next door neighbor, Sue, has three children. One summer day, she left her front door open and we were all standing out front visiting. Her three-year-old son, Ryan, ran in the house and locked himself in! She knocked and rang the bell, but Ryan must have thought it was funny, because he would not answer the door. No matter what she tried, he stayed in the house and wouldn't open the door. After a while, Sue got worried. She came over to my house to call her husband at work to bring home his key to let her in. Freddy, who was only ten at the time, heard what was going on and said: "I'll get him out!" Sue said she'd let him try. So, Freddy went to the phone and called Sue's house. Ryan answered the phone, of course. Freddy said: "Hi, Ryan! It's Freddy. Can I come over and play?" Ryan said: "Sure, come over!" When Freddy rang the doorbell, Ryan answered the door and let him in. Problem solved!

Magnetic Attractions: "You are needed!" Post this message and talk about how everyone – even the smallest child – has a role in the family.

Directions: Put yourself in another person's shoes. Literally. Trade shoes with someone in your family, and for a given amount of time, walk around the house trying to see things from that person's point of view. Does a child notice the dirty kitchen now that he's in mom's shoes? How does she feel about it? Does dad notice the broken yo-yo string when he's in the child's shoes? How can he help?

Responsibility

I feel myself so much a part of everything living that I am not
concerned with the beginning or ending of any one person in
this eternal flow.

— Albert Einstein

I've been seeing this bumper sticker around that really makes sense. It says: "Think Globally. Act Locally." You don't need to go and visit third-world countries to help humanity, although, if you want to do that, great! You can be of help right in your own neighborhood, your own community. Be aware of the opportunities and act on your instincts. Your heart is telling you to help! Everything we do makes a difference. There is no act of kindness too small. Start right where you are.

The best way to remake the world is by starting with yourself
and your internal world.

— Thom Hartmann

If we all got our acts together, think of what a great world this could be! It all starts with ourselves. We make the decision to live a spiritual life, to live fully with joy and gratitude, more people start making this decision and it snowballs from there. It shows in how we treat ourselves and others. It shows in how our planet functions and takes care of us. It's our responsibility to create the kind of life we want to live.

Let everyone sweep in front of his door and the whole world will be clean.

– Mother Teresa

Our acts of service and responsibility usually start small and build. When one person does it, it sets an example and other people want to do it, too! Good deeds become contagious. How fun!

It is not only what we do, but also what we do not do, for which we are accountable.

– Moliére

Just as we are responsible for our actions, we are responsible for our inaction. How many opportunities have we missed because of fear or anxiety? What haven't we done that needs to be done? If everyone thinks that it is up to someone else, nothing will ever get done. It takes all of us to get involved, we can't just sit on the sidelines.

 Magnetic Attractions: "Start where you are." Each family member do something small (but appreciated!) around the house: stock the toilet paper in each bathroom, bring out the garbage, put the dishes away, or sweep the front walkway.

Directions: Take responsibility! Make a list of what you and your family can do to help out and then do it. Look in the newspaper for ideas. In our local paper is a weekly feature called "involvement opportunities." It lists charities and organizations looking for volunteers. Check the bulletin boards at your church or schools. You are needed! Answer the call!

Community

'It was much pleasanter at home,' thought poor Alice, 'when one wasn't always growing larger and smaller, and being ordered about by mice and rabbits. I almost wish I hadn't gone down that rabbit-hole – and yet – and yet – it's rather curious, you know, this sort of life!'
　　　　　　 – Lewis Carroll, *Alice's Adventures in Wonderland*

There are a lot of benefits that come with all this responsibility when we leave the comforts of our homes and venture into the "outside" world. The world has a lot to offer us. There are mountains to climb, literally and figuratively! Opportunities abound. Life is a banquet, dig in!

Your good precedes you; it gets there before you do. But how to catch up with your good? For you must have ears that hear, and eyes that see, or it will escape you.
　　　　　　　　　　　　 – Florence Scovel Shinn

We need to be aware of all the good all around us. Whatever we focus on increases, so look for the good, embrace it and appreciate it. Look at all the people who are helping and join their ranks. Sure, there are problems, there are things that need to be fixed. But we have to see the good underneath, we have to see that the problems are worth fixing. It is all there, waiting for us. Our treasure is there for us to discover all along the way to getting There. You could get bummed out that the carpet is stained and needs to be replaced, but then you pull up the carpet and there is a beautiful hardwood floor underneath. These kinds of things happen all the time.

I joined our PTA to help my child's school. I ended up making some very close friends. Friends are a little nugget of gold that I didn't expect out of the experience, but I'm so glad I found them, or we found each other! When my mother re married, I didn't expect to get two great step sisters, but they were part of the package.

> *Thy friend has a friend, and thy friend's friend has a friend; be discreet.*
>
> – The Talmud

How many times have you heard: "It's a small world!" There are a lot of people in this world, yet it is a very small world indeed. From a spiritual perspective, we are all One, so there is no separation at all. But looking at us purely as individuals, it has been said that there is only a maximum of six degrees of separation between one person and any other given person anywhere in the world. We all know someone who knows someone! Remember that when you are out in the world, you represent not only yourself, but your family. Be responsible, serve your community with love.

> *If it hadn't been for neighbors, I'd have flunked my ink blot tests years ago!*
>
> – Erma Bombeck

I thank God for my neighbors! Sue, especially, has helped me out on numerous occasions. We watch each other's children, carpool when necessary, borrow sugar back and forth, and just generally live up to the ideal of suburbia at its best! Sue's son, Aaron, is Brian's best friend. Her husband, Fred, coached Brian's and Aaron's basketball team last year. It's so easy to feel isolated these days. Get to know your neighbors. Reestablish community.

 Directions: Subscribe to your local newspaper. Be aware of what is happening in your community. Get to know your local political representatives. Go to school board meetings. Participate in community events. Talk about what's going on with your children. Get them involved with groups like The Girl Scouts of America or Junior Achievement.

I wrote a song called "We Belong Together" that sums this all up pretty neatly. Here's a part of it:

> Just look at all we have,
> and all we have to give.
> It's more than we can hold,
> and more than can be told.
> But what matters most,
> in all of this,
> Is showing that we care.
> It's the way I feel about this world,
> Just knowing you are there.
> We Belong Together.
> We can close the world
> outside of us,
> And never be alone.
> And we can't get lost,
> in spite of us,
> Because where we are is home.

Directions: Turn to the person you're sitting beside on the school bus, your commute home, or your next airplane ride and make a connection. Choose to live your life alongside others.

7

Full Tank

Spirit is an invisible force made visible in all life.

– Maya Angelou

The world belongs to the energetical.

– Alexis de Tocqueville

We're on this journey, and something's got to keep us going. We've got three tanks that need to be filled: body, mind, and spirit. Keeping those tanks filled gives us plenty of energy to get There. Our bodies are maintained when we eat healthy foods and get sufficient exercise. Our minds are stimulated when we read and seek knowledge. Our spirits are nurtured with love, and by remembering our connection with God and nature.

Changes

We can not step twice into the same river, for other waters are continually flowing on.

– Heraclitus

Change is the one thing that never changes! Change is good for us, though we don't always recognize it at first. It shakes things up, forces us to think and adapt. Along the way to getting There, we can count on things changing and changing again. We'd be wise to remain flexible and resilient in the face of change. No one knows the importance of resiliency in the face of change better than a parent! Our children grow and change and go through stages and phases constantly! As they change, we must remain guided by our hearts, which may tell us to shift gears now and then.

Magnetic Attractions: "Change is good." Don't shy away from change. Let change happen. Post this when someone in the family is in a state of flux.

Ouvrez les yeux! Le monde est encore intact. Open your eyes! The world is still intact.

– Paul Claudel

We could spend a lot of time looking at all the problems in the world. And there are many people who do just that. But rather than focusing on problems, we could be dreaming up solutions.

Let's make a commitment to count our blessings and see all that is right in the world. We have a lot to be thankful for.

If we truly want to make the world a better place, we've got to start right here where we are. We can't change other people, but we can change ourselves and our own way of looking at things. One by one, family by family, we can be agents for change and make the difference that we want to see.

When we look at people, do we see height, weight, or hair color? Or do we look at them as spiritual beings? Remember, when we look into someone's eyes, we are looking at ourselves. We are mirrors of each other. We are One. As we get There, we understand this at a deeper level.

We can demonstrate this to our children in different ways as they grow. For example, if Becky hits Mark in the arm, Mark is hurt. But Becky is also hurt because she feels bad for causing Mark's pain. She didn't just hurt Mark, she hurt herself. Ten years later, when Becky gives Mark a ride home from school, he feels good that he got a ride, and she feels good that she helped a friend.

'Who are you?' said the Caterpillar. This was not an encouraging opening for a conversation. Alice replied, rather shyly, 'I – I hardly know, sir, just at the present – at least I know who I was when I got up this morning, but I think I must have been changed several times since then.'
– Lewis Carroll, Alice's Adventures in Wonderland

We all go through changes as we learn and grow. We're not the same people today that we were yesterday. No one knows this better than parents watching their children grow! Physically, our bodies are renewing with every breath. Mentally, we gain more knowledge through each new experience. And spiritually, we gain insight and wisdom each time we see God and connect with nature or each other. We are growing more and more towards realizing our true nature. We are all getting There.

Today, find a way to make changes in yourself instead of someone else. Sometimes the results are the same.

– Author unknown

We can't change other people, we can't change their behavior. We can only change the way we perceive the situation. How do we act? Do we overreact? Do we make demands? Are we judgmental? As parents, if our children are behaving badly, we need to approach the situation from a spiritual perspective. Is this bad behavior a call for love? Pay attention, communicate, find out what's going on and help your child modify his or her behavior.

Directions: Many of us make resolutions on New Year's Day. Of course, by about March, many of us have also forgotten what those resolutions are. When we sincerely want to make changes in our lives, we need to sit down and figure out exactly how we are going to do that. And we need to follow up with ourselves regularly. You don't need to wait until January to make a change. If there is something you want to change, make a pledge right here and right now that you will do it!

Freedom

'Why is it,' Jonathan puzzled, 'that the hardest thing in the world is to convince a bird that he is free, and that he can prove it for himself if he'd just spend a little time practicing? Why should that be so hard?'

– Richard Bach, *Jonathan Livingston Seagull*

Through prayer and meditation, we can begin to experience feelings of freedom, connection to God, Oneness. By bringing the peace we find in meditation into our active lives, we can begin to manifest this experience of freedom. The abundance of the universe is ours! Meditation is practice for feeling spiritual, for feeling our connection to God, in real life situations. The more we do it, the easier it gets.

A good relationship has a pattern like a dance and is built on some of the same rules. The partners do not need to hold on tightly, because they move confidently in the same pattern, intricate but gay and swift and free, like a country dance of Mozart's.

– Anne Morrow Lindbergh

It is important to allow freedom in our relationships, to recognize our interdependence without becoming too dependent. A person can't grow when he's being clung to, and the person doing the clinging can't grow, either! We do not need to hold on tightly – with our spouses, or with our children. We can't move forward if we're dragging each other down. Too much togetherness is stifling.

Allow for time alone as well as time together as a family. You'll have more to share when you come back together to compare notes.

 Directions: What makes you feel free? Roll down a grassy hill, run through an open field, or swing high until you feel you can touch the clouds. Breathe. Say: "I am free." This is a great family activity. Do a freedom-feeling family activity together. Go on a giant water slide, a roller coaster. Join arms at the elbow and spin in an open field! Take a Sunday afternoon trip to a park, beach, or open space, where everyone can run around, experiencing that feeling of freedom. Bring the dog, too, and let him chase after you!

Intention

All going forward comes from desire. Science today, is going back to Lamarack and his 'dint-of wishing' theory. He claims that birds do not fly because they have wings, but they have wings because they want to fly; result of the 'Push of the emotional wish.'

> – Florence Scovel Shinn

Where do we get motivation? From ourselves. Once we get motivated, we can set a goal. Intention is more than wishing, it's making a conscious decision and taking steps to reach that goal. We have the power to make things happen. We have the power to make changes in our lives.

> *'Would you tell me, please, which way I ought to go from here?' 'That depends a good deal on where you want to get to,' said the Cat.*
>
> – Lewis Carroll, *Alice's Adventures in Wonderland*

If we know where we're going, if we have that intention, then it is easy for us to make choices along the way. It's okay to keep changing your mind, but you'll get There a lot faster if you formulate a plan and stick to it. Make a map and follow it.

 Magnetic Attractions: "Dream solutions." Start a solutions network in your family. And learn to see not the limitations in the problem but rather the possibilities in the solutions.

One of Aesop's Fables tells about a big old cat who came to live in a big house. A family of mice had lived there for quite some time and were worried when they saw the cat had come to stay. Every time the mice headed to the kitchen for a bite of something to eat, the cat sent them scampering. "What will we do? We'll starve!" they cried, and decided to call a family meeting. They each took turns speaking, but no one could think of a plan. Finally, an uncle came forward and boasted that he had a plan that would work. He explained how a small bell attached to the cat's collar would warn all the mice of his approach. Patting himself on his own back for such an excellent idea, the uncle mouse sat down. The wise grand-father mouse stood up and said: "You are a very clever mouse to think up a plan like that! Now, tell us, are you brave enough to put the bell on the cat?" It's good to have a goal. If we also have a reasonable plan to get to that goal, and the courage to follow through with our plans, we will surely get There.

> *Why not spend some time in determining what is worthwhile*
> *for us, and then go after that?*
>
> – William Ross

Do we have our priorities straight? Do we know what we want? Do we know what is important? Our spiritual foundation helps us to answer these questions. Once we know that we are connected to God, nature and each other, that we are all One and all expressions of God, then we can go anywhere, easily, because we know that we're already There!

> *Let me tell you the secret that has led me to my goal. My*
> *strength lies solely in my tenacity.*
>
> – Louis Pasteur

Never give up. I've heard that from so many people in so many fields! Everyone gives the same advice, so there must be something to it. I heard Jay Leno interviewed one time and he was asked for the secret to his success. He said basically, "I never went away." He explained that stand-up comedy is a tough job — on the road, new material, and audiences all the time. A lot of guys just quit. But he didn't. He loved what he was doing, and he loves his job today. He's living his dream come true as host of The Tonight Show. Success is inevitable if you only keep going. Keep that goal in mind. Focus on the finish line, not on all the rocks and bumps between here and there. We can get there, we are getting There!

Magnetic Attractions: "Live your dream." Who in your family – immediate or otherwise – is living their dream? Share how that dream was realized.

Directions: Close your eyes and picture where you want to be one year from now. In five years? In ten? What steps do you need to take to get there? What changes would you make to how you're doing things now? Make a one-year plan, a five-year plan.

Manifestation

Believe that you have it, and you have it.

> – Latin proverb

If you really want something you can figure out how to make it happen.

> – Cher

The first step in achieving a goal is recognizing that it is possible to achieve it! Some people are afraid to have dreams because they sound too "pie-in-the-sky." If you think that they are, then they are. But if you think that you can do it, you can. Whatever we desire, we can achieve.

> *'There's no chimney,' Peter said; 'we must have a chimney.'*
> *'It certainly does need a chimney,' said John importantly.*
> *That gave Peter an idea. He snatched the hat off John's head,*
> *knocked out the bottom, and put the hat on the roof. The*
> *little house was so pleased to have such a capital chimney*
> *that, as if to say thank you, smoke immediately began to*
> *come out of the hat.*
>
> *– J. M. Barrie, Peter Pan*

The universe works with us to bring our dreams to fruition. We create our world. Things happen because we make them happen. God wants for us what we want for ourselves.

> *The spiritual attitude toward money is to trust in God for your*
> *supply. To keep your possessions, always realize that they are*
> *God in manifestation.*
>
> *– Florence Scovel Shinn*

God is everywhere, a part of everything . . . even money! Since God is limitless, our supply is limitless.

 Magnetic Attractions: "We create our world!" Remind the members of your family that their lives are what they make them. Set a good example by carving yourself a strongly-rooted, centered place in this world.

Directions: Make a treasure map. Everyone in the family can make his or her own. Put together a stack of old magazines and go through them with your children. Cut out pictures and words that represent your dreams and intentions. Paste them onto a piece of poster board to create a collage. Display your treasure map where you can look at it often.

Purpose

Mock Turtle said: 'No wise fish would go anywhere without a porpoise.' 'Wouldn't it really?' said Alice in a tone of great surprise. 'Of course not,' said the Mock Turtle: 'why, if a fish came to me, and told me he was going on a journey, I should say, 'With what porpoise?' 'Don't you mean "purpose?"' said Alice. 'I mean what I say,' the Mock Turtle replied in an offended tone.

– Lewis Carroll, Alice's Adventures in Wonderland

We have a purpose, even if we don't know it. It's no secret, really; scholars and sages have been telling us for centuries.

You may think that your purpose is to be a parent, or that your purpose is to run a company. But those are just choices we make to help us reach our purpose. Those are just things we do on the path to get There. We all have different goals, we all make different choices, but, bottom line is that we all have the same purpose. Our purpose is to know God, to rediscover our connection with the Divine. Our purpose is to love, grow, give, and gain wisdom.

Magnetic Attractions: "We each have a purpose."
Our purposes range from small to large – from making
sure the recyclables are put out on the right night to
contributing somehow to a cure for AIDS. Over
dinner everyone share a purpose.

> *'I myself own a flower,' he continued his conversation with
> the businessman, 'which I water everyday. I own three
> volcanoes, which I clean out every week. . . . It is of some use
> to my volcanoes, and it is of some use to my flower, that I
> own them. but you are of no use to the stars . . .' The
> businessman opened his mouth, but he found nothing to say
> in answer. And the little prince went away. 'The grown-ups
> are certainly altogether extraordinary,' he said simply, talking
> to himself as he continued on his journey.*
>
> – Antoine de Saint-Exupery, *The Little Prince*

In this story, the little prince is very wise, indeed. He sets off on a
journey to learn and he ends up teaching. As he gains knowledge,
he gives love, he is always working purposefully.

Knowing our purpose keeps us focused on what is important.
We can accomplish so much more when we keep this in mind.
When we come from a place of spiritual centeredness, we are
better people, and better parents.

*I wanted a perfect ending. Now that I've learned the hard
way that some poems don't rhyme and some stories don't
have a clear beginning, middle, and end. Life is about not
knowing, having to change, taking the moment and making
the best of it, without knowing what is going to happen next.
Delicious ambiguity.*

– Gilda Radner

Life is perfection, just the way it is.

 Directions: When going about chores and errands and
all the things you get done each day, keep in mind
your real purpose.

Solitude

*Woman must be the pioneer in turning inward for strength. In
a sense she has always been the pioneer.*

– Anne Morrow Lindbergh

In a family, it's usually, but not always, mom who is the spiritual
strength. Maybe because women tend to be more nurturing, we
have that motherly instinct. Mothers need to set the example for
their families and set time aside for themselves to fully experience
and express their spirituality. Women often tend to take care of
everyone else's needs first, and then maybe, if we have enough
energy, we do something for ourselves. Our own spiritual growth
needs to be a priority. We are better mothers, and better people,

when we give ourselves the time we need to connect with God and nature.

> *What a lovely surprise to discover how un-lonely being alone can be.*
>
> — Ellen Burstyn

Many parents, especially mothers, have been so caught up in doing things for the child all this time that they feel lost and lonely when by themselves. (Others feel great relief, at least for a little while!) The point is, it is okay to "do nothing." Sometimes "doing" all the time becomes an addiction and it is hard to overcome the feeling of "I should be doing something." When we're so busy doing: cleaning, shopping, working, fund-raising, etc. that we have no time for ourselves to just "be," then we're too busy. We need to say to ourselves: "Am I doing this for me, or for the sake of doing something when I really should be doing nothing?"

> But let there be spaces in your togetherness,
> And let the winds of heaven dance between you.
> Love one another but make not a bond of love:
> Let it rather be a moving sea between the shores of your souls.
>
> —Kahlil Gibran

> *Many a time I have wanted to stop talking and find out what I really believed.*
>
> — Walter Lippmann

We listen to people's opinions all day. How much time do we spend listening to our hearts? We really only answer to ourselves. Are we clear in our thinking?

> *But your isolation must not be mechanical, but spiritual, that is, must be elevation.*
>
> – Ralph Waldo Emerson

Solitude. Time alone. No television, no reading materials. Just peace and quiet. This is so difficult for some people. I think fear of boredom is really the greatest fear there is in today's population. The first few times spent in solitude may be difficult if you've never done it before. But you grow to appreciate and cherish this time the more you do it.

 Directions: If you had nothing to do, what would you want to do? (Cleaning out the closets doesn't count! This isn't an exercise to catch up on chores.) As parents, we probably can't remember back to a time when we had nothing that had to be done. So, if you can't come up with any ideas, borrow from your child's list: go skateboarding, eat a banana split, sleep in!

Your hearts know in silence the secrets of the days and the nights.

– Kahlil Gibran

We spend so much of our day in activity. We need to balance that activity with rest. With rest and activity we progress, and we will surely get There. Silence feeds our spirits. In silence, we find our strength, we feel our connection with the Divine.

All addictions come from looking for fulfillment outside of ourselves. Whether we're filling ourselves with food or drink, or filling our closets or filling our time, addictions take away from our spiritual growth. Addictions are distractions set up by our egos to keep us from God. Since we are the examples for our children, we are teaching them with our behavior. We need to make our spiritual growth a priority and not get caught up in doing everything except what we're really supposed to be doing, which is working on ourselves. This is something that we can begin to teach our children when they're quite young, so that they develop the habit as they grow.

Children are susceptible to addiction just as adults are. One of the more common addictions I've seen in children is an addiction to caffeine. Our children today are influenced by so many outside sources that as parents, we must be more aware than ever of the messages they are taking in. Soft drink companies are spending lots of money to get advertising into our schools and onto our playgrounds. They offer incentives like cash bonuses that go toward educational programs. But what are they really giving us? Our children are getting hooked on caffeine, an addictive drug. They will be spending their money to get their "fix" from these soft drinks maybe for the rest of their lives. These companies are targeting our youth the same way that the tobacco companies have been doing for years. They are even putting caffeine into traditionally noncaffeinated drinks like root beer, so we have to read the labels and be aware of what we are putting into our bodies.

Magnetic Attractions: "Honor your body." Talk about what you're putting into your bodies daily. Upgrade your fuel. The better care you take of your engine, the longer you will endure.

If you shut your eyes and are a lucky one, you may see at times a shapeless pool of lovely pale colours suspended in the darkness; then if you squeeze your eyes tighter, the pool begins to take shape, and the colours become so vivid that with another squeeze they must go on fire. But just before they go on fire you see the lagoon. This is the nearest you ever get to it on the mainland, just one heavenly moment; if they could be two moments you might see the surf and hear the mermaids singing.

– J. M. Barrie, *Peter Pan*

Our minds can take us anywhere. Our creative imagination knows no bounds. Spend time in silence and go where you want to go. It's a little vacation from your day!

 Magnetic Attractions: "Allow for time alone." Post this message especially when your family's pace is beyond hectic.

Directions: Make a date with yourself. Find a time and a place where you can be quiet. See how long you can go without the TV, radio, or telephone. Each time you do this should last a little longer. A peaceful environment is something that can be encouraged for everyone in the family to enjoy. Set aside some quiet time at home each day or each week.

Balance

The reverse side has also its reverse side.

– Japanese proverb

Balance is key. Balance activity and rest, balance work and play, balance family and career. Sometimes it seems like it is more of a juggling trick, but we can do it. Whenever we're out of balance, chances are it's because we've had too much activity, not too much rest! It's pretty easy to figure out how to bring ourselves back into balance.

Spiritually, opposites are found together. It's that seeming duality that confuses us, and makes us see two things as separate, rather than one. Look at examples of this in nature. Black and white are opposites, the zebra has black and white stripes. Is he a white horse with black stripes, or a black horse with white stripes? Both the black and the white make him the animal that he is. Here's another example you might find right in your own house: your cat. A cat has soft fur, it can be sweet and gentle. Yet the cat also has very sharp teeth, and beneath those soft pads on its feet, there are sharp claws! Sharp and soft are opposites, yet they are both the cat. That same duality exists within each one of us. As a parent, we are the disciplinarian and the nurturer. Whether we are mother or father, we contain aspects of both yin and yang, feminine and masculine. We don't have to be one or the other, we are both!

I now catch up with my good, for before I called I answered.

— Florence Scovel Shinn

Our good is waiting for us because our good is already there. We have it. We are There. We just don't know it yet! Maybe we just need to "lighten up" to tip the scales to a more balanced position. Balance togetherness with time alone. Let each person in your family have their personal time. A family that is spiritual individually is spiritual as a group. A spiritual family grows with love.

 Directions: Take your children to the park. Explain balance to a child when playing on a teeter-totter. Balance is also the principle used on doctor's scales. Find other examples and opportunities to discuss balance and how it applies to your family.

Energy is Eternal Delight

— William Blake

Energy is our fuel for this journey. There are a lot of things to stimulate us and help to get that energy up. When we feel passionately about something, we go after it. When things change, we need to think quickly and adapt. When we feel free, we are in balance, and our energy is free to flow. Flowing energy gives us a good attitude, a positive outlook on life, a love of living.

8

Happy
to Be Here

*What we teach our children is no different from what we must
keep teaching ourselves.*

– Deepak Chopra

The one thing that has more influence than anything else on our
well-being and spiritual growth is our attitude. Yes, it all comes
back to us once again. We can choose to have a good attitude. We
can choose to live a spiritual lifestyle. We can't get There without
making that choice!

Perception

Life does not consist mainly, or even largely, of facts and happenings. It consists mainly of the storm of thoughts that are forever blowing through one's mind.

– Mark Twain

Whatever is "out there" gets taken in by our eyes, registered in our brain, mulled around with our previous experiences with that thing, then given an emotion to attach to it. All of the thoughts in our mind go to interpret how we think or feel about something. Then something else comes along and that too is added to the store of knowledge. It's an amazing, ongoing process. But if we understand the process, we can change our thinking, and change our lives by changing how we look at things. How things are depends on how we see them.

We do not see things as they are. We see them as we are.

– The Talmud

Basically, we can't really take anything at face value, because face value means something different to each one of us, because we are different people with different experiences. For example: a cowboy hat may have no significance whatsoever to one person. To another, it represents a long lost grandfather. To another, it is the result of months of saved allowances. To another, it brings back memories of square dances with a sweetheart. We each bring our own meaning to the hat. We each see it a different way.

To a large degree "reality" is whatever the people who are around at the time agree to.

– Milton H. Miller

We do, however, share a certain public consensus. If a child plays a game of match the man with the hat, he would not match the businessman with the cowboy hat. Even if she had never had personal experience with a cowboy hat, she would know that it goes on a guy that looks like a cowboy, not a guy dressed in a business suit.

The way to change public perception is to change ourselves, one by one, through education. We all know that cowboy hats really could be worn in other situations. If a few successful businessmen started wearing them to the office, a trend might develop. Then it would be no big deal for more guys to wear cowboy hats, because public perception would have shifted and it would no longer be such an unusual thing.

When we first learned of the AIDS virus, many people were frightened. We didn't have enough information, so people filled in the blanks for themselves, coming from that place of fear. The result was that misinformation was taken as fact and public perception was that this was a "gay person's disease." When scientists and researchers learned more, they sought to educate the public. Given the correct information, public perception was changed, and we now understand that AIDS is an illness that can affect anyone. Spiritually, if it affects one of us, it affects all of us, because we are all ONE. With a spiritual attitude, we are free to make the changes necessary to eradicate this disease. The power of love can do anything.

If we could see the miracle of a single flower clearly, our whole life would change.

– Buddha

Change your thoughts, and in the twinkling of an eye, all your conditions change. Your world is a world of crystallized ideas, crystallized words. Sooner or later, you reap the fruits of your words and thoughts.

– Florence Scovel Shinn

You see the world as you believe it to be. If you believe that the world is in a mess, then that is what you will experience. If you believe that there is order in the world, that is what you will see. Knowledge is conviction, a statement stronger than belief. Know that your life is good and fruitful and it is. Know that your family is loved and protected, peaceful and together, and it is.

Wherever I go, there I am.

– Aristotle

We take our thoughts, beliefs, and experiences with us wherever we go. We carry them with us everywhere. If we are having problems in one city, we'll have those same problems in another city. If we are peaceful in one job, we will be peaceful in another job. Any problems we perceive outside the home will show up inside the home as well. We can't change our state of mind by changing our location or career. We can change our location or career, if that's what we want to do, by changing our state of mind first.

Magnetic Attractions: "I change my perception."
Practice changing your perspective about a recent difficult situation. Around the dinner table share the new way you each have of looking at your situation from another perspective.

> 'It was and is always your choice,'
> Said Gregory's still, calm little voice.
>
> —*David A. Anderson,*
> Journey to the Rainbow's End

Directions: What do you see? Take an item from one of your cupboards and ask family members to describe all the things they see. Write down all possible answers and find out how many you can come up with. For example, a cracker might also be: a square, a snack, a saltine, a carbohydrate, a toasty color, a food, a treat for a bird, or ten calories. All of these are a cracker, it's just that different people perceive things in different ways. When you've finished your lists, have a discussion about what each person learned.

Choices

*You have brains in your head. You have feet in your
shoes. You can steer yourself in any direction you choose.
You're on your own. And you know what you know. And
you are the guy who'll decide where you go.*

> – Dr. Seuss, *Oh, The Places You'll Go*

They can because they think they can.

> —Virgil

Our choices are like our steering wheels. We're holding the wheel,
we decide which way to go! Say: "I can because I think I can." Our
strength knows no bounds. It's the story of "The Little Engine That
Could" . . . because he thought he could!

*'Can they fly?' asked Roo. 'Yes,' said Tigger, they're very good
flyers, Tiggers are, Stornry good flyers. 'Oo!' said Roo. 'Can
they fly as well as Owl?' 'Yes,' said Tigger. 'Only they don't
want to.'*

> – A. A. Milne, *Winnie the Pooh*

Tiggers can do anything they choose to do, and we can, too.
What do you choose to do? Be mayor of the city? Earn a lot
of money? Tour museums in Europe? Start a charity for a
children's cause? Don't give away your freedom of choice. Don't
let anyone choose for you unless you are prepared to take
responsibility for that decision.

Magnetic Attractions: "Look within." Post this message when anyone in your family is making a difficult decision. Talk about what it means to look within.

Pain is inevitable. Suffering is optional.

– M. Kathleen Casey

We will have problems and frustrations and challenges in our life. That's the way it is, that's how we grow. It all comes with the territory. How we react to those challenges is our choice. How we deal with them is our choice. How we learn and grow from the experiences is our choice. Look within. Choose wisely.

We can help our children learn this by presenting their options to them. For example, if they are whining that they want you to buy them a toy, say: "Look at your choices here. You can continue whining, in which case we'll have to leave the store. You can ask politely and accept my answer. You can save up your allowance and get the toy for yourself. You can add that toy to your birthday list. Can you think of any other choices you have?" Allow them to make a choice and to live with the consequences of that choice.

> I've got to admit it's getting better,
> a little better all the time.
>
> —John Lennon and Paul McCartney, "Getting Better"

So I close in saying that I might have had a bad break, but I have an awful lot to live for. Today, I consider myself the luckiest man on the face of the earth.

– Lou Gehrig (1903-41)

Look at how Lou Gehrig chose to look at his situation. He faced his illness with courage and dignity and set an example for millions of Americans. How do you choose to perceive your situation?

Reminisce on a past family hardship and rethink the value of it. Despite its tribulations, how did it ultimately bring you closer together?

 Directions: Count how many choices you make in just one day. You choose what time to get up, what to have for breakfast, what kind of toothpaste to use . . . keep going. Among all these "little" choices are some big ones, too. When a car honks at you in traffic, how do you react? When your boss gives you a poor evaluation, how do you feel? When dinner is served and it is something you don't like to eat, how do you handle it? If you don't like the first choice you made, stop, adjust, and choose again. It's okay to change your mind to make a choice that is more spiritually in tune with where you want to be.

Optimism

I have noticed that folks are generally about as happy as they make up their minds to be.

– Abraham Lincoln

Optimists are healthier, happier, and live longer lives. Optimists are also more popular; people love being around people who are upbeat and positive.

Do you see the glass as half-empty or half-full? If you say it's half-full, then you are an optimist, and that's exactly what you want to be! Make up your mind to be happy and you will be. Let yourself be optimistic, let yourself be! Get into the happy habit. Smile. Laugh. Do things you like to do. Spend time with people you enjoy. Watch movies you love. Pretty soon you'll find yourself smiling and laughing without thinking about it!

Magnetic Attractions: "Be optimistic." Remember this message and practice seeing the good in a situation that at first glance seems unfortunate.

Spirit works through surprises and unexpected outcomes.

– Deepak Chopra

I expect the unexpected, my glorious good now comes to pass.

– Florence Scovel Shinn

Positive thinking can be stressful, it's as if you're trying to convince yourself that something is positive when you're not really sure. But there is a difference between positive thinking and positive knowing. Positive knowing is a confidence that things are handled and will turn out the way that they are supposed to. It's much stronger. It's knowing that you are fine regardless of the outcome of a situation. Practice positive knowing.

A man can succeed at almost anything for which he has unlimited enthusiasm.

– Charles Schwab

When we enjoy what we are doing, we accomplish so much more. Get into what you're doing. Build enthusiasm. If you see a spark, fan the flames. Encourage others, get enthusiastic about their projects. Encourage your kids to tackle school projects with vigor. Enthusiasm is contagious! It's also an essential ingredient for success.

Enthusiasm is the glory and hope of the world.

– Bronson Alcott

The words: "I'm bored" are not allowed in my house. If something is boring, it means that we are boring. We are projecting our own boredom onto things. Life is NOT boring! Life and everything in it is as exciting as we choose to make it! My kids know that the opposite of boredom is entertainment, and they have to find a creative way to entertain themselves! And they do! Try banishing the word "boring" from your house. Nurture enthusiasm instead.

 Directions: Generate enthusiasm. Pick a subject and have everyone think of ideas to get the rest of the group enthusiastic about it. Think of it as an advertising sales pitch. For example: coin collecting. Take five minutes or so for everyone to write down some notes, a few key words, and then take turns "pitching" coin collecting to the group. See who can creatively get everyone the most enthusiastic about it. "Major Investment Opportunity! Learn About the World! Don't miss out on being the first coin collector on your block!" Tear out ads from magazines and look at how these creative people generate enthusiasm for a product. How would you publicize your family? Have fun designing your own ad.

Fun

Life is too important to be taken too seriously.

– Oscar Wilde

Lighten up and live! Life is a journey. Why not make it a fun one? What makes it fun for you? Half the fun is finding out! Try new things, meet new people, make every day your own little party. Celebrate!

> *There is no pleasure in having nothing to do; the fun is in having lots to do and not doing it.*
>
> — John W. Raper

We all have obligations. Most of us love our obligations and would not trade them . . . we created them, after all. But, escaping from those obligations every once in awhile is important. When we get stressed-out, maybe we just need a day to cut loose, kind of "play hooky" for a few hours or so. When we enjoy ourselves, we accomplish more. So, we bring back a refreshed spirit to the office and meet our obligations with renewed appreciation.

> *One seal flipped George high into the air. Another seal caught him. All the seals poked their heads out of the water. They all wanted to play with George. They tossed George into the air and took turns catching him. George was having lots of fun. The audience went wild. It was the best show they had ever seen.*
>
> — Margret and H. A. Rey's *Curious George*

Curious George just wanted to play and have a good time. He enjoyed his life. The people who were supposed to be in charge of him thought he was getting into trouble and making a mess; those watching him wished they could do the same thing! George got away with a lot because he was a little monkey, but we humans can still cut loose and have fun now and then. One thing Curious George taught us was how to have fun.

Magnetic Attractions: **"Have fun!"** Post it: "Have fun!" Just do it!

Directions: Play Twister. Dress up in costumes and go visiting neighbors. Sing songs you learned in camp. Make a list of fun things you want to do, then do them!

Appreciation

Happiness does not consist of having what you want, but wanting what you have.

— Confucius

It has done me good to be somewhat parched by the heat and drenched by the rain of life.

— Henry Wadsworth Longfellow

Sometimes the trials and tribulations of life help us to appreciate the good times even more. We can't take life for granted. Like Longfellow, we can appreciate even the hard times for the strength that we get and the lessons that we learn from the experience.

My mother is always there for me when I need her . . . especially now that I've become a parent and I need her more than ever! She's a wonderful grandmother to the boys and she helps me out so much. Probably the lowest points in my life were when I had my two miscarriages. It was a very difficult experience to go through, both times, but my mom was really there for me. And even though it felt really terrible to have this happen, I know that I am a stronger and better person because of it. I have compassion for women who miscarry. I understand at a very deep level what they go through because I went through it. It was sad for our whole family, but I know that it brought us all closer together.

> *There is no one luckier than he who thinks himself so.*
>
> – German proverb

Every day can be your lucky day. It's all how you look at things. The day is what you make it. Do you see a rainy day, or do you see the flowers and the lawn being watered by God? Do you see traffic, or do you see an opportunity to listen to that book-on-tape you've been meaning to play? Make today your lucky day!

 Magnetic Attractions: "Choose a good attitude." Attitudes are there for the choosing. Post it and act it!

> *He dreams impractical dreams. He tries the patience of Job. But with his childlike trust and his zest for living, who am I to say that the drummer he marches to will not take him to the stars?*
>
> – Erma Bombeck

We all know a child who marches to the beat of a different drummer. So many times, teachers and parents try to make these kids conform to the norm. It's like the square peg, round-hole thing. What's best is to give love and encouragement. I'm sure that Steven Spielberg's mom, Bill Gate's mom, and Oprah Winfrey's mom would all say the same thing: They marched to a different drummer, and they turned out just fine, don't you think? Appreciate the unique qualities in your children and let them be the people they are.

Campfire Boys and Girls have organized "Absolutely Incredible Kids Day." On the third Thursday of every March, adults are encouraged to write letters of love, appreciation, and encouragement to children. Letters are something kids can save and read over and over again. It helps them to feel good about themselves knowing that someone cares.

 Magnetic Attractions: "Show you care." Take this opportunity to show your family you care. Hide a candy under someone's pillow. After a long day, offer a shoulder rub. Have a hot breakfast made on a Saturday morning before everybody wakes up!

Directions: Make the effort today to show someone how much you appreciate them. Write a letter or send a card. Find specific things to comment about. Be descriptive; use humor. It doesn't have to be long, just personal. Letter writing has become a lost art. Let's bring it back! Send handwritten thank-you notes. Make letter writing a habit. Kids love receiving mail, and they'll love sending it, too. Let them pick out their own stationery and get them started with their own address book.

Possibilities

If you can dream it, you can do it.

– Walt Disney

Walt Disney proved this time and time again. He dreamed up Disneyland! No one before had ever done anything like that. Walt Disney had a dream and he made it a reality. He created a whole world! He must have faced many people who told him that this was a ridiculous idea or that it was impossible to get it done. But Walt Disney followed his heart. He chose to dream and to act on his dream. There are unlimited possibilities open to us. What possibilities do you choose to see? Look within. Listen to your heart.

Don't believe what your eyes are telling you. All they show is limitation. Look with your understanding, find out what you already know, and you'll see the way to fly.

– Richard Bach, *Jonathan Livingston Seagull*

Magnetic Attractions: "Life is a journey." Where do you want to go? Plan a family day trip. Each member of the family jot down an idea for a day trip on a sticky note and post your ideas around the house.

Directions: Play "what if?" Think up fantastic possibilities for everyone in the house, for all sorts of scenarios. What if Brian got drafted into the NBA? Picture what life would be like for a nine-year-old professional basketball player! Make up stories about what would happen. What if Freddy's homemade rocket flew all the way to the moon? What if your class took a field trip to Mars? Come up with a bunch of your own and see what kind of stimulating conversation you can start by thinking about all the possibilities!

Self-Sufficiency

God gives the nuts, but he does not crack them.

– German proverb

Just as we need to know how to take care of ourselves, we need to teach our children how to be self-sufficient. This includes taking care of body, mind, and spirit.

Kids learn from us how to choose foods that are healthy, and how to exercise. They learn to read books that stimulate their intelligence and to engage in interesting conversations. And they learn the importance of meditation, prayer, and spending time with nature to feel our connection with God. We want them to become self-sufficient while they are with us, and to continue these practices when they are on their own.

> *'But how about my courage?' asked the Lion anxiously. 'You have plenty of courage, I am sure,' answered Oz. 'All you need is confidence in yourself. There is no living thing that is not afraid when it faces danger. True courage is in facing danger when you are afraid, and that kind of courage you have in plenty.'*
>
> – L. Frank Baum, *The Wizard of Oz*

Like the Cowardly Lion, the Tin Man, and the Scarecrow, we already have what we think we want. We have courage, we have a heart, and a brain! We just may not know it yet.

On the road to get There, we discover all the great qualities that are already within us. They are a part of us because we are ONE with God and ONE with each other. We see these qualities in God, we recognize these qualities in other people, and then finally we get around to seeing them in ourselves, too. And, like the Scarecrow and the Lion and the Tin Man, we are surprised to realize that they were there all the time.

> *Happiness is not the absence of problems, but the ability to cope with them.*
>
> – Author unknown

This is something we can teach our kids from very early on: Problems are a part of life, how we deal with them is our choice. We have the tools to cope with them spiritually. We need to use those tools, because when we do, the results make us much happier than when we don't.

 Magnetic Attractions: "You have options." Discuss important decisions with members of your family. Realize your options and make informed choices.

Say we're driving around and we suddenly get a flat tire. We have learned to pull over to the side of the road and put on our emergency lights. But then what do we do? What are our choices? What tools do we have to work with? My tools are my AAA card and my cell phone! I would call for help. Others might get a jack out of the trunk and change the spare tire themselves. That's the practical side of the problem.

But there's more to it than that. How do we react to the situation? What spiritual tools can we use to deal with the situation? What are our choices? We could get angry and frustrated and kick the tire. What good does that do? We could take a deep breath, center ourselves, and look for the good in the situation. Show gratitude: "Thank goodness I joined AAA!" Use the time waiting for help to meditate. Look at the scenery. Use this as an opportunity to learn how to change a tire. Meet new people! Look at this as an interesting story to share with friends at work. The choice is ours. The experience is good or bad depending on how we perceive it.

'Come, there's no use in crying like that!' said Alice to herself, rather sharply; 'I advise you to leave off this minute!' She generally gave herself very good advice (though she seldom followed it).

— Lewis Carroll, *Alice's Adventures in Wonderland*

How often do we follow our own good advice. We know what to do, we just have to do it!

 Directions: Get a piece of paper and write your name on it vertically, in all capital letters. For each letter in your name, write a positive quality that begins with that letter. Here's an example of one that Brian's friend Jake wrote for him:

> **B**rave
> **R**eally cool
> **I**ndependent thinker
> **A**wesome
> **N**ice

Then have family members do ones for each other. It's fun to see what everyone comes up with!

Our attitude sets the tone for our journey. We might as well make it a good one!

9

Round Trip Ticket

Gratitude is not only the greatest of virtues, but the mother of all the rest.

— Cicero

Think how wonderful life would be if gratitude were a part of our everyday routine. Whether we say grace at the dinner table, or prayers before bed, we can commit some time every day to recognizing the good in our lives and expressing our gratitude for it. When we bring our attention to the good things in our families, that good increases.

The deepest principle of human nature is the craving to be appreciated.

— William James

We really don't say "thank you" often enough. It's easy to take things for granted when we live with people and we spend as much time together as a family does. Be grateful every day for your family, and let them each know, individually and as a group, how much you appreciate them. Let's thank God every day, too.

> Our family spends a lot of time talking about gratitude, especially at Thanksgiving. Here are some prayers that my sons Freddy and Brian wrote, with my help, to say at Thanksgiving dinner:
>
> Thank You for this food.
> Thank You for our home.
> Thank You for our family,
> We know we're not alone.
> You're with us now as we say thanks,
> You're with us everyday.
> For this we're thankful most of all
> You're here to guide our way.
>
> We're thankful for this day at home
> And all the people we love.
> Our hearts are filled with gratitude
> For Your blessings from above.
> Thank You for our animals,
> Our neighborhood and school.
> May we be giving thanks each day
> For all we are and all we do.

A simple grateful thought towards heaven is the most complete prayer.
– Gotthold Ephraim Lessing

Spiritual practice is not just setting aside time during the day to meditate or to be spiritual. It's going about the day with a spiritual attitude, an attitude of gratitude! We can give thanks all along the way: when we find a good parking place, when there's no line at the market, when the mail comes without any bills, or when the kids come home with good grades. Life is wonderful! Notice this and give thanks for it!

It takes awareness to remember that life
is a gift, however overwhelmed we may be by other thoughts
and pursuits.

– Deepak Chopra

When we are aware, gratitude fills our hearts. And when we are grateful, we are awake and aware. This is a great way to live life, a great way to travel!

Thanks to flowering of white moon
and spreading shawl of black night
holding villages and cities together

—*James Berry*

Things can happen all around us, yet we can remain centered, in spirit, and filled with gratitude.

Got no checkbooks, got no banks.
Still I'd like to express my thanks -
I've got the sun in the mornin'
And the moon at night.

—*Irving Berlin,* "I Got the Sun in the Morning"

Magnetic Attractions: "Have an attitude of gratitude." Be grateful today for small things. List some of those small things on sticky notes and stick them around the house.

We can all experience the beauty of our universe, wherever we may be. This is something we all share. It's the same moon all over. And it is ours! Be grateful!

Gratitude is the sign of noble souls.

– Aesop

Directions: Play the Grateful Game. Gather the family around the table. Starting with the youngest, go clockwise around the table having each one say one thing that he or she is grateful for. Each person has just ten seconds to come up with something, and once something is said, it can't be repeated by anyone else. Everything is fair game from "I am grateful for the sun," to "I am grateful for video games," (a big one in our house) to "I am grateful that mom bought Girl Scout cookies." Whatever it is must be in the positive (not something you are grateful didn't happen) and must be the truth (don't say you're grateful for peanut butter if you don't like peanut butter.) In the Grateful Game, everyone's a winner, but the last person left in the game after everyone else has run out of things to say gets first dibs on dessert.

Forgiveness

Love truth but pardon error.

– Voltaire

The weak can never forgive. Forgiveness is the attribute of the strong.

— Mahatma Gandhi

Children are really good at forgiving. They don't hold a grudge. One time a friend of Brian's popped a blister on Brian's hand. It hurt, and Brian cried. His friend felt bad, but Brian just looked at him and said: "That's okay. I know you didn't mean it." They were off playing in no time like nothing happened.

Everybody makes mistakes. It's okay to make mistakes. If someone hurts us, whether we think they meant to or not, it is so important that we forgive them. By hanging on to hurt and anger, we only hurt ourselves. By forgiving someone else, we are really forgiving ourselves because we are all One. What happens to one of us, happens to all of us. The universe is affected by each of our actions. At the same time, by offering forgiveness, we're bringing more love to the universe. Forgiveness is a gift we give ourselves and the world.

If we can genuinely honor our mother and father, we are not only at peace with ourselves but we can then give birth to our future.

— Shirley Maclaine

Not everyone has had a perfect childhood. Many of us came from families of divorced parents. Some suffered physical and/or emotional abuse in their homes. But we can't hold on to the past. We need to let go and forgive. We need to live our lives in this moment in time and not let the past steal our present. Most parents just do the best job that they can at any given time.

The key to change . . . is to let go of fear.

— Rosanne Cash

When we let go of fear in any form (anger, hurt, anxiety) we allow in love. There is lots of room for love! To let go of fear, forgive!

Magnetic Attractions: "Look for opportunities!" Now's the time to wash yourself clean of fear and resentment. Grab the moment and let go of the anger.

If you can't change your fate, change your attitude.

— Amy Tan

Our attitude is one thing that we can change. It is our choice. We can change our whole life, which direction we're taking on the path, just by letting go and changing our attitude.

Directions: Write a letter to someone who has hurt you. Kids can do this, too, if they are hanging on to some resentment. Get it all out on paper, let all your feelings pour out. Then crumple up the paper and throw it in the fireplace! As the paper goes up in flames, release your hold on those negative emotions. Let go! Forgive. It's over and done with. Move on.

Magnetic Attractions: "Forgiveness is a gift we give ourselves." Let go of a grudge and feel the wings of forgiveness lift you above and beyond the situation.

Through forgiveness the thinking of the world is reversed. The forgiven world becomes the gate of Heaven, because by its mercy we can at last forgive ourselves. Holding no one prisoner to guilt, we become free.

— A Course in Miracles

Forgive and be free.

Peace of Mind

Let one therefore keep the mind pure, for what a man thinks, that he becomes.

— The Upanishads

Whatever you think about, whatever you pay attention to, becomes more important in your life, and increases. Keep your thoughts on good things. Focus on what is important: the Divine.

The happiest moments of my life have been the few that I have passed at home in the bosom of my family.

— Thomas Jefferson

Have faith that everything works out for the best. When we are not attached to a situation, it can work itself out. When we're hanging on too tightly, the knots can't loosen. Allow God to be present in all situations.

> *Nothing in life is more exciting and rewarding than the sudden flash of insight that leaves you a changed person, not only changed but for the better.*
>
> – Arthur Gordon

The road to get There is filled with these flashes of insight. That's what keeps us going, looking for the next one. It's thrilling, really. Spiritual growth is the best feeling!

> *Every man must find his own philosophy . . . his attitude toward life.*
>
> – Lin Yutang

> *Traveler, there is no path; paths are made by walking.*
>
> – Spanish saying

Again, it's all up to us. No one can make us do anything or feel anything. No one can change us, we can only change ourselves. We find our own philosophy, we discover ourselves and our own spirituality.

Magnetic Attractions: "Follow your heart." Sometimes your heart knows where you want to go before you do. Share stories after dinner with your family about pivotal instances in your life where you listened to your heart and were led in the right direction.

Once we're seasoned travelers, there are a few lessons we've learned that we want to pass on to others on the journey to help them along. Call them "Rules of the Road":

1. Pack Light. Don't carry the heavy burden of a guilty conscience; be honest. Keep life simple; you don't NEED too many things to weigh you down. Always carry a full tank of love in your heart and you'll have the strength to pull any load.

2. Help Out. Give "roadside assistance" whenever you're needed and chances are that another traveler will be there to help you when you need it, too. Contribute to the community with your time, talent, and money to help keep the roads smooth and the scenery beautiful. You'll enjoy the journey that much more.

3. Explore. Learn the lay of the land. Find out where you want to go and your mind will take care of how to get you there. The fastest, easiest way is not necessarily always the best way. Don't be afraid to ask for direction; you can get good tips from people and books, but always follow your heart and allow for serendipity.

4. Take Care of Your Equipment. Take care of your self: body, mind, and spirit. You'll be putting a lot of miles in, so make sure you're in good shape. Eat right, exercise, keep a regular routine, and avoid toxins such as tobacco and caffeine. All parts in this engine are connected, so keep a good attitude, balance your activities, and spend time with yourself in silence.

5. Enjoy the Journey. Live in the present moment. Stop and smell all the flowers, not just the roses. Learn to embody even the "thorns" of the roses in your life. Be aware of and appreciate all the sights and sounds and opportunities presented to you all the time.

> So let us become Miracle Conscious; [if we] prepare for miracles, expect miracles, we invite them into our lives.
>
> – Florence Scovel Shinn

We have an opportunity right now to bring spirituality and spiritual thinking into our lives and the lives of our children. Let's make this a growing trend. One person at a time, one family at a time, we will become one great big spiritual world filled with loving, fulfilled people!

 Directions: Look for opportunities to grow spiritually and take them!

About the Author

Like many children do, Lisa Marie Nelson (then Granich) had imaginary friends when she was growing up in Northern California. Now she believes these friends to have been angels, guiding her way on the spiritual path.

An award-winning producer and songwriter, Lisa Marie established Bright Ideas Productions in 1990 to provide original, upbeat entertainment for children. She has created products in nearly every media, including the "Positive Music for Today's Kids!" audio series and the "Karate for Kids" home videos. Her music videos currently air on The Learning Channel. She has co-authored, with Louise Taylor, *The Healthy Family Handbook* (Tuttle, 1997).

Lisa Marie appears frequently on national television, taking a light-hearted look at parenting today. She tackles a wide range of topics, and is known for her unique spin and creative solutions. She also covers family and lifestyle stories for both broadcast and print media.

Lisa Marie works with several nonprofit groups and serves on the Professional Advisory Board for CH.A.D.D. (Children and Adults with Attention Deficit Disorders) of California Pacific Region. She holds a Bachelor of Science degree in Sociology from the University of California, Los Angeles. She is married, has two children, and the family lives in Southern California.